20 Egyptian Songs
to Learn and Sing

T0352129

20 Egyptian Songs to Learn and Sing

An Easy Way to Learn Egyptian Colloquial Arabic

Bahaa Ed-Din Ossama

Tessa Grafen

The American University in Cairo Press

Cairo   New York

The author and publisher are grateful to the following for permission to use material in this book: Ms. Amina Jahine for the lyrics in chapters 15, 16, and 17 and Ms. Mai Mansour for the lyrics in chapters 7, 12, and 14. Every reasonable effort has been made to contact the copyright holders. We apologize and thank any authors or copyright holders whom we have not been able to properly acknowledge. If a work in copyright has been inadvertently included, the copyright holder should contact the publisher.

First published in 2021 by
The American University in Cairo Press
113 Sharia Kasr el Aini, Cairo, Egypt
One Rockefeller Plaza, 10th Floor, New York, NY 10020
www.aucpress.com

Dar el Kutub No. 13351/18
ISBN 978 977 416 905 2

Dar el Kutub Cataloging-in-Publication Data

Ossama, Bahaa Ed-Din
    20 Egyptian Songs to Learn and Sing: An Easy Way to Learn Egyptian
    Colloquial Arabic / Bahaa Ed-Din Ossama.—Cairo: The American University
    in Cairo Press, 2018.
        p.   cm.
        ISBN 978 977 416 905 2
        1.   Arabic language – Dialects – Egypt
        2.   Arabic language – Conversation and phrase books
        492.75

1 2 3 4 5   25 24 23 22 21

Designed by David G. Hanna
Printed in the United Kingdom

Contents

Introduction

20 Egyptian Songs was written as a celebration of the spoken Egyptian dialect and to grant it the importance it deserves as a fundamental part of Egypt's illustrious heritage. It includes popular songs covering a wide variety of themes and genres—from romance to patriotism, and from philosophy to social criticism—all of which have been performed by famous singers in Egypt. Some were recorded at the beginning of the twentieth century while others were released in the last few years. Altogether, the chapters provide a rich insight into modern Egyptian culture.

This book provides the reader with the chance to study popular songs at a beginner's level, either through self-study or in a classroom context, and as needed, the author has added *tashkil* (the short vowels) to the words in order to help the student with both comprehension and pronunciation. There are twenty lessons, broken into five levels according to difficulty. Each four lessons cover a level. Each lesson focuses on a different song and provides the song lyrics together with a vocabulary list and notes explaining the historical and cultural background of the song, before proceeding to exercises that allow students to practice the vocabulary and grammar they have just learned. At the end of the book there is a grammar section that covers some grammatical constructions used in the songs and explains them in simple terms.

Although the songs have been ordered according to their difficulty, a chronological list has been provided for students who wish to clearly trace the evolution of Egyptian music. Students can study them in the order of the textbook, individually, or in any order they choose.

In order to get the most out of this book, students should already be familiar with the basics of Arabic such as the alphabet, the numbers, and gendered nouns. From this book, they will learn the foundations of Egyptian Arabic, including the present and future tenses, the imperative and subjunctive, active and passive participles, and ordinal numbers. It should give students a firm grasp of the fundamentals of Egyptian grammar and help them to communicate and express themselves in the Egyptian dialect.

ترجمة لنصوص الأغاني

قائمة الأغاني

الأغاني بالترتيب الزمني

١

الحـــــرام

٢٠١١

كلمات: منتصر حجازي - ألحان وغناء: دينا الوديدي

Dina El Wedidi first released "الحرام" (The forbidden) on YouTube in 2011. The song was later included in her 2014 album "تـدوّر وترجـع" (You search and come back). In this song, El Wedidi criticizes religious extremists who consider different forms of art, such as singing, inherently sinful and therefore needing to be banned. "الحـرام" became a hit and spearheaded a trend of songs criticizing the current conditions which stifle personal expression in Egypt.

الحَرام هُوَّ الحَرام يا عَم يا بتاع الكَلام
الحَرام هُوَّ الحَرام يا عَم يا بتاع الكَلام
الحَرام مُش إنِّي أَغَنِّي
الحَرام مُش إنِّي أَحب
الحَرام هُوَّ الكَلام اللي نُصُّه يا عَم كِدْب
ده الحَرام هُوَّ الكَلام اللي نُصُّه يا عَم كِدْب
الحَرام مُش هُوَّ فَنِّي
الحَرام مُش إنِّي أَحسَ
الحَرام هُوَّ الكَلام اللي نُصُّه يا عَم كِدْب

المفردات

not	مش
to sing	غنى، يغني
lie	كدب
to feel	حس، يحس
half	نص ج. إنصاص

ملاحظات

١- الحرام

Forbidden

(حرام) means "forbidden" and indicates a sinful deed in Islam, such as drinking alcohol or engaging in extramarital sex.

٢- بتاع الكلام

Someone who is all talk

(بتاع) indicates ownership or possession. It agrees in gender and number with the noun being possessed, and is used with a possessive suffix or a noun (that indicates who or what is the owner of the possessed object). The following shows the different forms of (بتاع) when the noun being possessed is masculine:

بتاعي – بتاعَك – بتاعِك – بتاعه – بتاعها – بتاعنا – بتاعكو – بتاعهم

Feminine:

بتاعتي – بتاعتَك – بتاعتِك – بتاعته – بتاعتها – بتاعتنا – بتاعتكو – بتاعتهم

Plural:

بتوعي – بتوعَك – بتوعِك – بتوعه – بتوعها – بتوعنا – بتوعكو – بتوعهم

These examples show how (بتاع) is used with a suffix:

This book is mine, not yours.	الكتاب ده بتاعي مش بتاعك.
My car is outside.	العربية بتاعتي بره.
Was your bag lost?	الشنطة بتاعتك ضاعت؟
Your two books are in the room.	الكتابين بتوعكو في الأوضة.

(بتاع) can also be used with a noun to indicate certain characteristics or interests of a person, or even what they do for a living, as in this song with (بتاع كلام), meaning someone who is all talk or who makes things up.

Some other examples include:

A greengrocer	بتاع الخضار
A fruitseller	بتاع الفاكهة
A ladies man	بتاع بنات
A troublemaker	بتاع مشاكل
The marrying type	بتاع جواز

٣- الحَرام هُوَّ الكَلام اللي نُصُّه يا عَم كِدْب

This talk of haram, half of it is a pack of lies, my friend
(يا عم) is a familiar form of address, that can be used informally between friends or acquaintants. Although (عم) literally means "uncle," (يا عم) in English could correspond to "my friend," or "brother," "dude," or "mate" (in British parlance). (يا) is the vocative and is used before the name or title of the person being addressed. It is like the old-fashioned "O" in English, but is commonly used in the spoken Egyptian dialect.

التدريبات

1. Tick the sentence that makes sense according to the song.

( )	الحرام إني أغني، الحرام إني أحب.	١.
( )	شرب الخمرة حرام في الإسلام.	٢.
( )	أي نوع من الفن حرام في الإسلام.	٣.
( )	بتاع الكلام هو الشخص اللي بيتكلم كتير.	٤.

2. Choose the correct word to complete the sentence:

(بتاعي - بتاعتي - بتوعي)	القلم .... فوق المكتب.	١.
(أستاذ - عم - دكتور)	يا ....، عايز بخمسة جنيه عيش.	٢.
(بتوع - بتاع - بتاعة)	.... الفاكهة في شارعنا اسمه أحمد.	٣.
أنا شفت مسرحيات كتير قديمة وجديدة. أنا راجل .... مسرح. (بتوع - بتاعة - بتاع)		٤.

3. Write a sentence with each of the following words:

....
....
....
....

4. Find an example of the following from the song:

أفعال مضارعة من غير (ب)

....

5. Describe this picture, using the words you have learned:

....
....
....
....

٢

نـــور العيـــن

١٩٩٦

كلمات: أحمد شتا - ألحان: ناصر المزداوي - غناء: عمرو دياب

This Spanish-style song is sung by one of the most famous singers in Egypt and the Arab world, Amr Diab. It is influenced by European music and uses the guitar and accordion, which are not traditional Arabi c instruments.

In the video, Diab revealed a new look, with short, slicked-back hair. A craze for this hairstyle swept Egypt along with the so-called "Spanish hijab," a new way of wearing the headscarf that is similar to the way the dancers in the video tied their bandanas.

The video was also a dramatic step away from the studio-based clips of the early nineties, moving toward the more adventurous videos seen on music channels today.

حَبيبي يا نور العين يا ساكن خَيالي
عاشق بَقالي سنين ولا غيرك في بالي
حَبيبي يا نور العين يا ساكن خَيالي
عاشق بَقالي سنين ولا غيرك في بالي
حَبيبي حَبيبي حَبيبي يا نور العين
يا ساكن خَيالي
أَجْمَل عُيون ف الكون أنا شُفْتَها
الله عَليك الله عَلى سِحْرَها!
عُيونَك مَعايا، عُيونَك كفاية
تنَوَّر لَيالي
حَبيبي حَبيبي حَبيبي يا نور العين

يا ساكِن خَيالي
قَلبَك نَاداني وقال بِتْحِبّني
الله عَليك الله طَمَّنْتني!
مَعاك البِداية وكُلّ الحكاية
مَعاك للنِّهاية
حَبيبي حَبيبي حَبيبي يا نور العين

المفردات

darling, beloved	حَبيب ج. حَبايب
light	نور
eye	عين ج. عُيون
to live in, dwell	سَكِن، يِسْكُن
imagination	خَيال
to adore, love	عَشِق، يِعْشَق
no one but you	ولا غيرك
apart from	غير
mind	بال
pretty, beautiful	جَميل/ة ج. جُمال
universe	كون
to see	شاف، يُشوف
magic	سِحْر
enough	كفاية
to light up, illuminate	نَوَّر، يِنَوَّر
night	ليلة ج. ليالي
heart	قَلْب ج. قُلوب
to call	نادى، يِنادي
to say	قال، يِقول
to love	حَبّ، يِحبّ
to reassure	طَمَّن، يطَمَّن
beginning	بِداية ج. بِدايات
story	حكاية ج. حكايات
ending	نِهاية ج. نِهايات

ملاحظات

١- يا ساكن خيالي

You who resides in my fantasies

(سـاكن) here refers to a girl, even though the masculine form for the active participle has been used (rather than the feminine form سـاكنة). This is a common practice in Arabic songs and poetry, and you will find many songs using masculine nouns, verbs, adjectives, and pronouns to refer to or address women. Maybe because Arabs considered the word "حبيـب" as masculine and they felt it is sufficient to refer to the beloved one no matter their gender.

٢- عاشق بقالي سنين

I've been in love for years

This expression (بقالـي) is made up of (بقـى لـ + ضميـر) and is used to express a duration of time that has passed, and can be similar to the English prepositions "for" and "since."

When you add a suffix to the word (بقـى), as with any other noun that ends with the alif maqsura (ى), the alif maqsura changes into a regular alif (١).

In the song, it is added to the preposition (لـ) and the first-person pronoun. This is how other pronouns can be added :

بقالها	هي	بقالي	أنا
بقالنا	إحنا	بقالك	إنت
بقالكو	إنتو	بقالك	إنتي
بقالهم	هم	بقاله	هو

Here are some examples of this expression:

I have been living in the United States for ten years.

أنا عايش في أمريكا بقالي عشر سنين.

She has left her country for two years now.

هي سايبة بلدها بقالها سنتين.

My son has been playing football for three years.

ابني بقاله تلات سنين بيلعب كورة.

How long have you been playing the piano for?

إنتي بقالك قد إيه بتلعبي بيانو؟

How long have you been in Egypt?

إنتو بقالكو قد إيه في مصر؟

We have been living here for five years.

إحنا بقالنا خمس سنين ساكنين هنا.

My God!

This expression is used when admiring or praising someone, and can have the meaning of "well done," as in the following sentences:

إنت حلّيت في الامتحان النهارده كويس جدًا، الله عليك!

You did really well in the exam today, well done!

الله عليكي يا مريم! ده أحسن ماتش لعبتيه في حياتك!

Well done, Maryam! That is the best game you've ever played!

التدريبات

1. Tick the sentence that makes sense according to the song.

١. أجمل عيون للكون أنا شفتها.   (   )

٢. عيونك معايا، عيونك كفاية.   (   )

٣. معاك البداية وكلي الحكاية.   (   )

٤. عاشق بقالي سنين وأنا غيرك في بالي.   (   )

٥. قلبك ناداني وقال تحبني.   (   )

2. Correct the underlined word in these sentences:

١. لازم بناكل في المطعم الإيطالي قريب.

٢. أختي بتحب بتسمع موسيقى كلاسيك.

٣. المسلمين مش كلوا لحم الخنزير.

٤. إنتو تتفرجوا على حاجة دلوقتي؟

3. State what the pronouns in the following sentences are referring to.

١. الله على سحرها.

٢. ولا غيرك في بالي.

٣. قال بتحبني.

٤. يا ساكن خيالي.

٥. أنا شفتها.

4. Choose the correct word from the brackets.

١. الكاتب لازم يكون .... واسع.   (خياله – قلبه – نوره)

٢. إنت .... عليك لمّا كلمتني في التليفون.   (حبيتني – شفتني – طمّنتني)

٣. كل الرّز اللي اشتريناه مش .... عشان الحفلة كبيرة قوي.   (كفاية – معايا – حكاية)

٤. ماما، ممكن تحكي لي ....؟   (قلب – حكاية – خيال)

٥. أنا ساكن في مصر .... لي عشر سنين.   (سحر – نور – بقى)

٦.   ممكن .... الأوبرا الأسبوع ده.   (بنروح – نروح – هنروح)

٧.   عايز .... جاكيت جديد قريب.   (أشتري – باشتري – هاشتري)

٨.   الشمس .... اليومين دول حوالي الساعة ٦.   (بتطلع – طلعت – تطلع)

٩.   مين .... عصير الجوافة هنا؟   (يحب – بيحب – هيحب)

5.   Write a sentence with each of the following words:

سحر – طمَن – حكاية – بداية – نهاية – خيال

....

....

....

....

6.   Find examples of each of the following from the song:

– فعل مضارع مع (بـ)

....

– فعل مضارع بدون (بـ)

....

– أفعال ماضية – صفة على وزن أفعل

....

7. Describe this picture, using the words you have learned:

....
....
....
....
....

٣

أنا هويت

١٩٢٣

كلمات: محمد يونس القاضي – ألحان وغناء: سيد درويش

This is one of the most popular songs in Egypt. It was composed and sung by the prominent Egyptian musician and singer Sayed Darwish, shortly before his death in 1923. He continues to be revered by Egyptians, and his songs, especially this romantic one, have been covered by many artists. Sayed Darwish is considered the creator of dramatic expression in Egyptian singing, by making the music and the performance flow in harmony with the subject and the sense of the lyrics. The situation before him was not like this. It was possible then that the lyrics would be sad and the music happy, and the performance did not always express the lyrics.

أنا هويت وانتهيت وليه بقى لوم العذول
يحب إني أقول يا ريت الحب ده عني يزول
ما دمت أنا بهجره ارتضيت خلي بقى اللي يقول يقول
أنا وحبيبي في الغرام مافيش كده ولا في المنام
أحبه حتى في الخصام وبعده عني يا ناس حرام
مادمت أنا بهجره ارتضيت مني على الدنيا السلام

المفردات

to love	هوى، يهوى
to end	انتهى، ينتهي

why	ليه
blame	لوم
rebuker, critic	عذول ج. عواذل
to like, love	حب، يحب
to say	قال، يقول
I wish, if only	يا ريت
to go away from, leave, abandon	زال، يزول عن
abandonment, separation	هجر
to be satisfied, content	ارتضى، يرتضي
to let	خلى، يخلي
darling, beloved	حبيب ج. حبايب
love	غرام
dream	منام
even	حتى
fights, disagreements	خصام
distance	بُعد
people	ناس
life, world	دنيا
peace	سلام

ملاحظات

١- ليه بقى لوم العذول

Why would I blame . . .

The meaning of the word (بقى) depends on the context and it can be used to give emphasis to a question, as in this song. Here are some examples:

So why did you buy this watch, then?

إنت ليه اشتريت الساعة دي بقى؟

So where are you from, Sara?

إنتي منين بقى يا سارة؟

So why should I go to bed early today?

أنام بدري النهارده ليه بقى؟

So who was it that brought these books?

مين بقى جاب الكتب دي؟

٢- ما دمت أنا بهجره ارتضيت

As long as I have accepted her leaving me

(ما دام) is a verb that means "as long as (he/it)." It is conjugated like the verb (قال), but can be used without conjugation, or as a connector as shown below:

As long as you are staying here, I will come to stay with you.

ما دمت هتقعد هنا هاجي أقعد معاك.

As long as you want to travel, you must get a passport.

ما دام عايز تسافر لازم تعمل باسبور.

I will not come tomorrow, as long as it is a day off.

أنا مش هاجي بكرة ما دام بكرة أجازة.

٣- خلي بقى اللي يقول يقول

Let those who talk, talk

(خلي) is the imperative form of (خلى، يخلي), which means (to let), while (بقى), as shown above, is used to emphasize the imperative sentence.

Here are some more examples of (بقى), this time used as in a command:

Do your homework!

اكتب بقى الواجبات بتاعتك!

Give me this book!

هاتي الكتاب ده بقى!

Eat the food before it gets cold!

كلوا بقى الأكل قبل ما يبرد!

(اللي) is the relative pronoun most commonly used in Egyptian dialect. It is only used after nouns with the definite article or a possessive suffix. It does not have different forms and can be used for masculine and feminine, singular and plural, human and non-human, as we see in these sentences:

The pen that I bought is for ten pounds.

القلم اللي اشتريته بعشرة جنيه.

The teacher who teaches us Arabic is called Mostafa.

المدرس اللي بيعلمنا عربي اسمه مصطفى.

The country (which is) next to us is Libya.

الدولة اللي جنبنا هي ليبيا.

The girls who I met are studying here.

البنات اللي قابلتهم بيدرسوا هنا.

٤- مافيش كده ولا في المنام

There is nothing like this, not even in a dream
(مافيش كده) means "there is nothing like this," while (ولا) means "not even."

٥- بعده عني يا ناس حرام

His distance [from me] is haram
(حـرام) in addition to its original meaning of something forbidden in a religious sense, this word can also mean something that is a pity or a shame, as in the following examples:

It is a pity to throw away this carpet, it's beautiful.

حرام ترمي السجادة دي، دي شكلها جميل.

It would be a shame if we did not see this movie in the cinema.

حرام مانشوفش الفيلم ده في السينما.

٦- مني على الدنيا السلام

I am at peace with the world
This is an old-fashioned expression conveying the idea of being at peace with people and life.

التدريبات

١.   حط علامة صح أو غلط قدام الجمل دي.
أ- العذول يحب إني أقول يا ريت الحب عني يزول.   (   )
ب- الشاعر مش بيحب حبيبه لما بيخاصمه.   (   )
ت- حرام يعني حاجة غلط في الدين بس.   (   )
ث- بعده عني يا ناس عادي.   (   )

٢.   اختار الإجابة الصحيحة من بين الأقواس.
أ- الفيلم .... بعد ساعتين.   (هوى - انتهى - بقى)
ب- .... السنة الجاية أشتري عربية.   (يا ريت - حرام - مافيش كده)
ت- مابحبش .... كتير مع أصحابي.   (الحرام - الخصام - السلام)
ث- .... الكلب يمشي شوية كل يوم.   (بقى - خلِّي - ليه بقى)
ج- إمبارح شفت .... غريب وأنا نايم بالليل.   (منام - سلام - حرام)

ح‌‌‌‌‌‌‌‌‌– .... تضرب إنسان أو حيوان.   (الحب – حرام – العذول)

خ‌– الشخص اللي بيحسد الناس اللي بيحبوا بعض اسمه .... (المنام – العذول – الحرام)

د‌– .... يعني الحب.   (العذول – الغرام – الخصام)

ذ‌– كل تونة .... الدكتور قال لك لازم تاكل سمك.   (مافيش كده – ما دام – ارتضيت)

ر‌– دلوقتي فيه .... بين مصر وإسرائيل.   (سلام – دنيا – عذول)

٣.   حطّ الكلمات دي في جمل من عندك:
هويت – حرام – خلّي – خصام – غرام – ما دام – يا ريت

٤.   وصّل الكلمة بعكسها.

سلام	عدو
بُعد	حلال
حرام	قرب
انتهى	حرب
حبيب	ابتدى

٥.   استخرج من النص:
٣ أفعال ماضية

....
....
....

٣ أفعال مضارعة

....
....
....

فعل أمر

....

....
....
....
....
....

٤

حِلْوة الدُّنيا سُكَّر

١٩٦٩

كلمات: محمد حمزة – ألحان: بليغ حمدي – غناء: شادية وسمير صبري

This is an English–Arabic song from the Egyptian movie "نص ساعة جواز" (Marriage for Half an Hour) starring Shadia, Rushdi Abaza, and Magda El-Khatib, written by Ahmed Ragab and based on the play *Cactus*, produced by Ramsis Naguib, and directed by Fatin Abdel Wahab. The song encourages us to put ourselves first in order to enjoy life to the full and, in the film, the lead character performs this song to her lover to make him jealous. Singer Samir Sabri, who spoke English having worked for a European program on Egyptian radio, added the English lyrics during rehearsals. The poet and the movie director welcomed the additions, and the song was ultimately performed in both languages.

Lovely! How the world is lovely!
Live now and tell me you love me.
Lovely! How the world is lovely!
Live now and tell me you love me.
One night . . . let us live for one night.
Kiss me and hold me so tight.

سُكَّر والله الدُّنيا سُكَّر
اسْهَر حبّ الدُّنيا أَكْتَر
سُكَّر والله الدُّنيا سُكَّر
اسْهَر حبّ الدُّنيا أَكْتَر
ليلة واتْمَتَّع لَك ليلة

ليلة عيش دي الدُنيا جَميلة زَي السُّكَر

Lovely! How the world is lovely!

Live now and tell me you love me.

Lovely! How the world is lovely!

Live now and tell me you love me.

One night . . . let us live for one night.

Kiss me and hold me so tight.

ياما ضَحّينا وياما

خَدْنا إيه من كِلْمة ياما

إلّا لوم وعتاب وَمَلامة

إلّا نار وَعَذاب وَنَدامة

ليلة هاتْمَتَّع لي ليلة

ليلة عيش دي الدُنيا جَميلة زَي السُّكَر

المفردات

sugar	سُكَر
the world	دُنْيا
to stay up (or out) late	سِهِر، يِسْهَر
to enjoy	اتْمَتَّع، يِتْمَتَّع
to sacrifice	ضَحَّى، يِضَحِّي
to take	خَد، ياخُد
word	كِلْمة ج. كَلِمات
except	إلّا
blame	لوم
blame	عتاب
reproach	مَلامة
fire, pain	نار
torture	عَذاب
regret	نَدامة

ملاحظات

١- ليلة واتمتع لك ليلة

Live for one night

The preposition (ـل) can be added to direct object pronouns (i.e., ـي، ـك، ـه، ـها) and used after the verb to emphasize a reflexive action (e.g., to wash oneself). It is often used in Arabic to convey the idea of having time to do something enjoyable for oneself, for example:

I'm going to read my book then go to sleep.

أنا هاقرا لي كتاب وأنام.

Go outside and get yourself some fresh air to wake you up.

روح شم لك شوية هوا عشان تصحى.

She went into her bedroom to have a little sleep.

دخلت أوضتها تنام لها شوية.

We went downtown to have a stroll for a couple of hours.

رحنا نتمشى لنا ساعتين في وسط البلد.

He went into the kitchen to get himself something to eat.

دخل المطبخ ياكل له حاجة.

التدريبات

١. حطّ علامة صحّ أو غلط قدّام الجمل دي.

أ- الدَنيا وحشة قوي زي السكر.   ( )

ب- عشان الدَنيا جميلة أحسن نسهر.   ( )

ت- أحسن حاجة إننا نضحي.   ( )

ث- اللوم والعتاب والملامة تقريبًا نفس الحاجة.   ( )

ج- المغنية قررت تستمتع بحياتها.   ( )

٢. كمّل الجمل دي بكلمات من عندك.

أ- السَوق ده أنا عارفاه كويس جدًا .... لفيت فيه قبل كده.

ب- كتر .... بين الأصحاب بيبوظ الصَداقة.

ت- لو النَاس مش .... في الحياة كانت هتبقى مملَة.

ث- معظم المصريين مابيناموش .... العيد.

ج- باحبَ .... في إسكندرية في الصَيف عشان جوَها أحسن من القاهرة.

٣. اختار الكلمة الصحيحة من بين الأقواس.

أ- الدّب قاعد على الجليد .... ببرودة التّلج. (بيضحّي - بيتمتّع - بيعيش)

ب- القمر بيكون بدر .... ١٤ في الشّهر العربي. (ندامة - ملامة - ليلة)

ت- إمبارح .... لحد السّاعة تلاتة بالليل. (سهرت - ندمت - عشت)

ث- اللبن ده بارد قوي، حطّه شوية على .... (اللوم - النّار - اليوم)

ج- .... قريت كتب في مكتبة الجامعة القديمة. (لي - دي - ياما)

٤. حطّ الكلمات دي في جمل من عندك:

لوم - عذاب - ياما - نار - اتّع

....

....

....

٥. استخرج من النص:

٤ أفعال أمر

....

....

....

....

فعلين ماضيين

....

....

فعل في المستقبل

....

....
....
....
....
....

٥

يا حُبِّنا الكِبير

٢٠١٣

كلمات: عبد الفتاح مصطفى – ألحان: رياض السنباطي – غناء: أم كلثوم ومحمد منير

This is one of three patriotic songs included in this book. In it, the singer
addresses his homeland, Egypt, calling it his "great love." It was originally
sung by Umm Kulthum in 1965, and was unusual for its time in that it
focused on the country itself rather than on the Egyptian president, Gamal
Abdel-Nasser. In 2013, a remix of the song, featuring abridged lyrics and
vocals by Mohamed Mounir, was a hit. This is the version included below.

يا حُبِّنا الكِبير والأوَّل والأَخير
يا ضامِمْنا تَحْت ضِلَّك وف خيرَك الكتير
يا حَبيب كُلّ الحَبايب الحاضِر واللي غايب
مَلايين لكن ف حُبَّك كُلّنا أَهْل وَقرايب
تجمَعْنا كلِمتَك، تدفَعْنا ثَوْرتَك
والفَرْحة فَرْحتَك والنَّصْرة نَصْرتَك
وف أعيادَك نِهنّي ونْغَنّي غِنْوتَك
تعيش وتِسْلَم
تَعيش وتِسْلَم
تِعيش وتِسْلَم يا وَطني

المفردات

big, large   كِبير ج. كُبار

first	أَوَّل، أُولى
last	أَخير، أَخيرة
joining, uniting, embracing	ضامم ج. ضامّين
under	تَحْت
shadow, shade	ضلّ
resources, goodness	خير
many, much	كتير ج. كُتار
who, which	اللي
present	حاضر ج. حاضْرين
absent	غايب ج. غايْبين
million	مِلْيون ج. مَلايين
but	لَكن
family	أَهْل ج. أَهالي
relative	قَريب ج. قَرايب
to bring together, collect	جَمَع، يِجْمَع
to push, motivate	دَفَع، يِدْفَع
revolution	ثَوْرة ج. ثَوْرات
joy	فَرْحة
victory	نَصرة
feast, holiday	عيد ج. أعياد
song	غِنْوة
to live	عاش، يِعيش
to be safe	سِلِم، يِسْلَم
homeland, motherland	وَطَن

ملاحظات

١ - تجمعنا كلمتك، تدفعنا ثورتك

Your word unites us, you revolution moves us forward
The poet is referring to the 1952 revolution against the Egyptian monarchy and the British occupation, in which the Egyptian military overthrew King Farouk I and declared Egypt a republic in 1953.

التدريبات

١. حطّ علامة صحّ أو غلط قدّام الجمل دي.

أ- الشاعر اتكلّم عن ثورة ٢٥ يناير في الأغنيَّة. ( )

ب- المصريين أهل وقرايب في حب مصر. ( )

ت- آلاف من المصريين بيحبُّوا بلدهم. ( )

ث- المصريين اللي عايشين في مصر بس همَ اللي بيحبُّوها. ( )

٢. كمَّل الجمل دي بكلمات من عندك.

أ- الملك فاروق ساب مصر بعد .... ١٩٥٢.

ب- .... كلهم عايشين في بلدي إنجلترا، أنا بس اللي عايش في مصر.

ت- عرفت معنى .... لما قابلت حبيبتي في الجامعة.

ث- في مصر أربع ....، عيدين مسيحيين وعيدين إسلاميين.

ج- زميلي اللي في الفصل كان .... إمبارح عشان تعبان.

٣. اختار الكلمة الصحيحة من بين الأقواس.

أ- حبيبي آدم هو الحب .... في حياتي. (الكبير والكتير – الأول والأخير – الحاضر والغايب)

ب- عدد المصريين دلوقتي فوق ال ١٠٠ .... نسمة. (مليون – ألف – ملايين)

ت- كل الأطفال .... في حفلة عيد الأم. (حبوا – عاشوا – غنوا)

ث- هارجع أرض .... الشَّهر الجاي إن شاء الله. (الثورة – الوطن – الخير)

ج- .... الأخيرة في بلدنا كانت سنة ١٩٩١. (الفرحة – النَّصرة – الثَّورة)

٤. حطّ الكلمات دي في جمل من عندك:

أول – قرايب – أهل – أعياد – غنَّى – وطن

....

....

....

....

....

....

٥. وصَّل الكلمة بعكسها.

حاضر	فرَّق
أول	صغير
حب	كره
كبير	أخير
جمع	غايب

٦. استخرج من النّصَ:

٣ اسم فاعل

....

....

....

٦ أفعال مضارعة

....

....

....

....

....

....

....
....
....
....

٦

خَلّيك فاكِرْني

١٩٩٩

كلمات: عادل عمر – ألحان: عمرو مصطفى – غناء: عمرو دياب

"خَلّيك فاكِرْني" (Remember me) is one of the most popular songs by the Egyptian pop superstar Amr Diab. It was released in his 1999 album "قمرين" (Two moons), and included a duet by Diab and the famous Algerian artist Cheb Khaled, titled "قلبي" (My heart).

خَلّيك فاكِرْني

ياللي بْجَمالك وبْعُيونَك دول آسِرْني

خَلّيك فاكِرْني

وإنْ حَسّ قَلْبَك يوم بقَلْبي ابْقى زورْني

دانْتَ ف عينيَا كُلّ اللي ليَّا

فَرْحة شَبابي والدُنْيا ديا

أوّل ما شُفْتَك

لَمّست قَلْبي بنَظْرة واحْدة نسيت جراحُه

لَقيتَك إنْتَ أَجْمَل حكاية حُبّ نَسّتْني اللي راحوا

ماتْغيبِش عَنّي

وخَلّي قَلْبَك لَوْ ناديت ييجي لي تاني

داحْنا اللي بينا الحُبّ كُلّه وعُمْر مَرّ مَعاك ثَواني

دانْتَ ف عينيَا كُلّ اللي ليَّا

فَرْحة شَبابي والدُنْيا ديا

خَلّيك فاكِرْني

ياللي بْجَمالك وبْعُيونَك دول آسِرْني

خَلّيك فاكِرْني

وإنْ حَسّ قَلْبَك يوم بقَلْبي ابْقى زوِرْني
دانْتَ ف عينيَا كُلَ اللي ليَا
فَرْحة شَبابي والدُّنْيا ديا
خَلِّيك فاكِرْني

المفردات

this, these	دَه، دي، دول	
to capture	أسَر، يأْسِر، أسْر	
joy	فَرْحة	
youth	شَباب	
this	ديا = دي	
as soon as	أوّل ما	
to see	شاف، يشوف، شوف	
to touch	لَمَس، يِلْمِس، لَمْس	
look	نَظْرة ج. نَظَرات	
to forget	نِسي، يِنْسى، نِسْيان	
wound	جرْح ج. جِراح	
to find	لَقى، يِلْقى	
to make someone forget	نَسّى، يِنَسّي	
to be absent	غاب، يِغيب عن، غِيب	
to come	جه، ييجي، مِجِيّ	
age	عُمْر ج. أعْمار	
to pass	مَرّ، يِمُرّ، مُرور	
second (time)	ثانِية ج. ثَواني	

ملاحظات

١- خَلّيك فاكِرْني

Remember me

(خَلّي) is the imperative form of (خَلّى، يخَلّي), and it means to keep, to let, or to leave (something as it is), depending on the context.

Keep the cheese in the fridge.

خلّي الجبنة في التلاجة.

Keep the door open.

خلّي الباب مفتوح.

Leave the book on the table.

خلّي الكتاب فوق الترابيزة.

Additionally, the structure (خلي + pronoun + adjective), when used as a command, means to continue to do something:
Don't forget (literally: continue to remember) the book.

خلّيكو فاكرين الكتاب.

Stay asleep until I come.

خلّيك نايم لحد ما آجي.

Keep your swimming suit on (literally: continue to wear) as we'll go in the water again.

خلّيكي لابسة هدوم البحر عشان هننزل تاني.

٢- أول ما شفتك لمست

(أول ما) means "as soon as" and it can be used with any tense:
As soon as I woke up, I took a shower.

أول ما صحيت خدت دش.

As soon as I mention you, people start to laugh.

أول ما باجيب سيرتك الناس كلها بتضحك.

As soon as I arrive, I will call you.

أول ما هوصل هكلمك.

٣- أجمل حكاية

(أجمل) is the superlative adjective of (جميل).

التدريبات

١.   حط علامة صح أو غلط قدام الجمل دي.

أ- الشاعر بيطلب من حبيبته تنساه. ( )

ب- الشاعر حبها من أول نظرة. ( )

ت- ماكانش بينهم قصة حب. ( )

ث- الشاعر وحبيبته دلوقتي مع بعض. ( )

ج- الشاعر كان عنده قصص حب قديمة. ( )

٢.   كمل الجمل دي بكلمات من عندك.
أ- .... بكرة، تعالى عشان محاضرة بكرة مهمة جدًا.
ب- الأولاد في المدرسة النهارده كانوا عايزين يسمعوا .... علاء الدين والمصباح السحري.
ت- لما إنتي .... عليا، أنا ماسمعتكيش عشان كنت في أوضتي والباب مقفول.
ث- .... الإنسان دلوقتي وصل ١٠٠ سنة أو أكتر.
ج- الويتر قال لي .... وجه بعد ربع ساعة.

٣.   اختار الكلمة الصحيحة من بين الأقواس.
أ- .... عارف أن الشنط الجلد أغلى من الشنط العادية.   (خليك – أول ما – خلي)
ب- .... باباكي يتصل بيا ضروري عشان عايز أكلمه.   (خلي – لست – نسيت)
ت- .... عرفت إنه نجح في الامتحان حضنته.   (لقيتك – أول ما – خليك)
ث- بعد ما اتجوزت وخلفت حسيت إن عمري .... بسرعة قوي.   (أسر – مر – دانت)
ج- .... واحدة في الامتحان عرفت إنه صعب.   (ناديت – خلي – بنظرة)

٤.   استخرج من النص:
اسم فاعل
....

٧ أفعال ماضية
....
....
....
....
....
....
....

فعل مضارع فعل أمر
....

فعل نهي
....

صفة أفعل التفضيل

....

جملة شرط

....

٥. حط الكلمات دي في جمل من عندك:

جمال – لمست – لقيتك – نسَى – مرَ – فرحة – شباب

....

....

....

....

....

٦. وصل الكلمة بعكسها.

جم	نسَى
فكَر	فرحة
حضر	راحوا
قبح	غاب
حزن	جمال

٧. اوصف الصورة دي.

....

....

....

....

....

٧

أَنا باعشَق البَحْر

٢٠٠٠

كلمات: عبد الرَّحيم منصور – ألحان: هاني شنودة – غناء: محمد منير

This romantic poem was originally sung by Nagat El Saghira in 1979. It expresses the poet's love for the sea, the sky, and the road, comparing them to his beloved. The version included here is a cover by Mohamed Mounir, one of the most popular Egyptian singers of all time. Mounir's music has a universal appeal that seems to transcend age and class, earning him the nickname "The King" in Egypt.

أَنا باعْشَق البَحْر

زَيَّك يا حَبيبْتي حَنون وساعات زَيَّك مَجنون

ومهاجر ومسافر

ساعات زَيَّك حَيْران وساعات زَيَّك زَعْلان

ساعات مَلْيان بالصَّبر

دَه أَنا باعشق البَحْر

أَنا باعْشَق السَّما

عَلشان زَيَّك مسامْحة مَزروعة نُجوم وفَرْحة

حَبيبة وغَريبة

علشان زَيَّك بعيدة وساعات زَيَّك قَريبة

بعيون مُتْنَغِّمة

ده أَنا باعْشَق السَّما

أَنا باعْشَق الطّريق

لإنُّه فيه لُقانا وفَرْحنا وشَقانا

أَصحابْنا شَبابْنا

فيه ضِحْكت دُموعْنا وفيه بكِيت شُموعْنا
وضاع فيه الصَّديق
ده أَنا باعْشَق الطَّريق
أَنا باعْشَق البَحُر وباعْشَق السَّما وباعْشَق الطَّريق
لإنُّهم حَياة وإنْتي يا حَبيبتي إنْتي كُل الحَياة

المفردات

sea	بَحْر ج. بُحور، بحار
as, like	زَي
affectionate	حَنون/ة
sometimes	ساعات
crazy, mad	مَجنون ج. مَجانين
migrating	مهاجر ج. مِهاجْرين
traveling	مِسافر ج. مِسافْرين
confused, perplexed	حَيْران ج. حَيْرانين
sad, upset	زَعْلان ج. زَعْلانين
full of	مَلْيان
patience	صَبْر
sky, heaven	سَما
forgiving	مِسامح ج. مِسامْحين
planted	مَزْروع
star	نِجْم ج. نُجوم
strange	غَريب ج. غُراب
far, distant	بعيد ج. بُعاد
near, close	قُرَيَّب ج. قُرَيِّبين
melodious	مِتْنَغَّم
way, road	طَريق ج. طُرُق
because	لإن
meeting	لُقى
joy, gladness	فَرَح
suffering, trouble, pain	شَقى
friend	صاحب ج. أَصْحاب

youth	شَباب
to laugh	ضِحك، يِضْحَك
tear	دَمْعة ج. دُموع
to cry, weep	بَكى، يِبْكي
candle	شَمْعة ج. شُموع
friend	صَديق ج. أَصْدِقاء
life	حَياة
all, whole of	كُل

ملاحظات

١- مهاجِر ومسافِر

Migrating and traveling
These are the active participles of (هاجِر) and (سافِر).

٢- ساعات زيك حَيْران وساعات زيك زَعْلان

Sometimes confused like you, sometimes sad like you
(زَعْلان) and (حَيْران) belong to the group of adjectives which end in the syllable (ان). They usually refer to human beings, animals, or plants and they express feelings or states of being. For example:

Sad	زعلان	Cold	بردان
Happy	فرحان	Hot	حرّان
Awake at night	سهران	Hungry	جعان
Confused	حيران	Full	شبعان
Impassioned, furious	هيجان	Thirsty	عطشان
Lazy	كسلان	Bored	زهقان
Tired, unwell	تعبان	Sleepy	نعسان
Wilted	دبلان		

Note that (بـردان) and (حـرّان) cannot be used to describe objects; (بـارد) and (سـخن) are used instead while (بـرد) and (حـر) are often used to describe the weather.

٣- ساعات مليان بالصبر

Sometimes full of patience

The adjective (مليان) follows the same pattern explained above and it can describe people and in this case means chubby. It can also be used to describe objects and it means full in this case; for example:

الكوباية مليانة دلوقتي.

٤- علشان زيَّك مسامحة

(علشان), (عشان) meaning "so," "because," or "as."

بعيون متنغمة

With melodious eyes

(متنغم) is the active participle of a passive verb (اتنغم).

التّدريبات

١. حطّ علامة صحّ أو غلط قدّام الجمل دي.

أ- البحر ساعات بيكون حنون وساعات بيكون مجنون.   (   )

ب- حبيبة الشَّاعر ساعات بتكون حيرانة وساعات بتكون زعلانة.   (   )

ت- ساعات السَّما بتكون بعيدة وساعات بتكون قريبة.   (   )

ث- الشَّاعر مابيحبّش صديقه.   (   )

ج- الأرض مزروعة نجوم وفرحة.   (   )

٢. كمّل الجمل دي بكلمات من عندك.

أ- عايزنا نروح السينما الساعة ١ بالليل في الشتا يا .... ؟

ب- إنت قاعد لوحدك كده ليه؟ إنت .... ولا إيه؟

ت- الجنينة بتاعتنا كلها .... خضار وفاكهة.

ث- معلش، اتأخرت عشان .... كان زحمة.

ج- باحب أكلم صاحبي على السكايب (Skype) عشان باخد رأيه في حاجات كتير.

٣. اختار الكلمة الصحيحة من بين الأقواس.

أ- الأسد مشهور بالقوة، والجمل مشهور .... (بالصبر - بالطريق - بالصحرا)

ب- أنا .... مش عارف أدرس في أنهي جامعة.			(زعلان - مليان - حيران)

ت- أجمل حاجة في السما			(الشموع - النجوم - الفرحة)

ث- حبيبتي وقفت جنبي كتير في .... ودلوقتي إحنا أسعد زوجين.			(هنايا - الطريق - شقايا)

ج- ليه يا حبيبتي .... ؟ مش قادر أشوف دموعك.			(بتبكي - حيرانة - زعلانة)

٤.	حطّ الكلمات دي في جمل من عندك:

مجنون - مسافر - صبر - حبيب - غريب - باعشق - شموع - دموع - صديق - أصحاب - شباب

....
....
....
....
....
....
....
....
....
....
....

٥.	استخرج من النص:

كل الصفات - فعل مضارع - ٣ أفعال ماضية - اسم فاعل - اسم مفعول

....
....
....
....
....
....
....
....
....
....
....
....
....
....
....

....
....
....
....
....

٨

أهو ده اللي صار
١٩١٩

كلمات: بديع خيري - ألحان وغناء: سيد درويش

This patriotic and political song by Sayed Darwish is widely considered to be a masterpiece. It was first performed in the 1920s, when Egypt was still a British colony. In the song, Darwish calls on Egyptians to stop blaming each other for the country's problems and to work together in order to wrest control of its vast resources from the British and to provide for themselves independently. Many artists have performed covers of this popular song.

أهو ده اللي صار وآدي اللي كان
مالَكْش حَقّ مالَكْش حَقّ تلوم عَلَيّا
تلوم عَلَيّا إزّاي يا سيدْنا
وخير بلادْنا ماهوش ف إيدْنا؟
قوللي عَن أَشياء تفيدْنا
وبَعْدَها ابقى لوم عَلَيّا
مَصْر يا أَمّ العَجايب
شَعْبِك أَصيل والخصْم عايب
خَلّي بالك مِن الحبايب
دول أَنْصار القَضية
وبدال ما يِشْمَت فينا حاسد
إيدَك ف إيدي وقوم نجاهد
واحنا نِبْقى الكُلّ واحد
والأَيادي تكون قوّيَة

المفردات

to become, be	صار، يصير
right	حق ج. حقوق
how	إزاي
sir	سيد
is not	ماهوش
thing	شيء ج. أشياء
to benefit	فاد، يفيد
oddities, miracles	عجايب (مفرده عجيبة)
people	شعب ج. شعوب
noble	أصيل/ة
opponent, enemy	خصْم ج. خُصوم
to censure	عاب، يعيب، عيب
instead	بدال ما + فعل مضارع
(you) take care of	خلي بالك
defender, protector	نصير ج. نصراء
cause, issue	قضية ج. قضايا
to rejoice in someone else's misfortune	شمت، يشمت، شماتة
to envy	حسد، يحسد، حسد
hand	إيد ج. أيادي (مؤنثة)
to rise, set out, start, undertake	قام، يقوم
to endeavor, strive, fight for	جاهد، يجاهد، جهاد

ملاحظات

١- أهو ده اللي صار وآدي اللي كان

This is what happened, and this is where we are
(أهو) and (آدي) have almost the same meaning which is "there/here it is."
(أهو) has a feminine form (أهي) and a plural form (أهم) and can come before

or after the noun which it refers to, while (آدي) has only one form and only comes before the noun.

There he is, the teacher who will teach us Arabic.

أهو ده المدرس اللي هيعلمنا عربي.

Here is the new bag.

أهي دي الشنطة الجديدة.

There are the Brazilian students.

الطلاب البرازيليين أهم.

There's the school bus. On you get!

آدي أتوبيس المدرسة، ياللا اركبه.

٢- مالكش حق

You have no right

We can negate pronouns—especially if they are connected to prepositions—by adding them between (ما) and (ش) like in the past tense verbs. For example:

أنا	مانيش	ليا	ماليش
إنت	مانتَش	ليك	مالكش
إنتي	مانتيش	ليكي	مالكيش
هو	ماهوَش	ليه	مالوش
هي	ماهيش	ليها	مالهاش
إحنا	ماحناش	لينا	مالناش
أنتو	مانتوش	ليكو	مالكوش
هم	ماهمش	ليهم	مالهمش

This book has no use (or, the book is useless).

الكتاب ده مالوش لزمة.

Aren't you afraid of lions?

مانتش بتخاف من الأسد؟

We don't understand anything at all.

ماحناش فاهمين حاجة خالص.

You have no right to blame me.

مالكش حق تلوم عليا.

التدريبات

١. حط علامة صح أو غلط قدام الجمل دي.

أ- الشاعر بيقول إن خير بلادنا في إيدينا. ( )

ب- الشاعر عايز يتكلم في حاجات مفيدة. ( )

ت- الحاسدين بيشمتوا في الناس. ( )

ث- في رأي الشاعر، مصر بلد عجيبة. ( )

ج- الشاعر بيطلب من مصر تخلي تخلي بالها من الأجانب. ( )

٢. كمل الجمل دي بكلمات من عندك.

أ- لازم .... بلادنا يكون كله لينا.

ب- الدرس ده مالوش لزمة، مافيهوش حاجة ....

ت- .... من صحتك، ماتشربش سجاير كتير.

ث- إنت اتعاملت مع أي .... تاني غير المصريين؟

ج- .... في إيدي كده، ساعدني.

٣. اختار الكلمة الصحيحة من بين الأقواس.

أ- لازم تاخد .... بنفسك، عشان ماحدش هيجيبهولك. (تلوم - حقك - يشمت)

ب- دراسة اللغات الأجنبية .... كلنا. (بتفيدنا - بتلومنا - بعدها)

ت- غلط .... الطفل على كل حاجة بيعملها. (تشمت - تلوم - بقى)

ث- اتفرج معايا على الفيلم ده وبعده .... نام لو عايز. (بقى - بدال - لوم)

ج- .... ما تشتري هدوم دلوقتي وهي غالية، اصبر بعد شوية هتكون أرخص. (نجاهد - بدال - صار)

٤. استخرج من النص:

٥ أفعال مضارعة

....

....

....

....

....

....

اسمين فاعل

....

....

فعلين أمر

....
....

٥. حط الكلمات دي في جمل من عندك:

أهو – آدي – خير – حق – بدال ما – أصيل – قضية

....
....
....
....
....
....
....

....

....

....

....

الدُّنيا ريشة في هَوا

١٩٥٧

كلمات: مأمون الشناوي – ألحان: محمد عبد الوهاب – غناء: سعد عبد الوهاب

This is a lighthearted song about change and instability. The poet calls on us to accept life as it is and to not despair in times of trouble, as life is full of contradictions and transformations.

الكورس: الدُّنيا ريشة في هَوا، طايْرة بغير جناحين

إحْنا النَّهازْده سَوا وبُكْرة هنْكون فين؟

في الدُّنْيا في الدُّنْيا

المطرب: ياما ناس بتتْقابل من غير مَعاد يجْمَع بينْهُم

وناس بتتْحايل على الفُراق بيْبعد عنْهُم

الكورس: مين ضَمّهُم بإيديه واتْفَرّقوا حَواليه؟

المطرب: سَبَب لُقاهم إيه؟

الكورس: إيه؟

المطرب: وكان فُراقُهم ليه؟

الكورس: ليه؟

الدُّنيا ريشة في هَوا، طايْرة بغير جناحين

إحْنا النَّهازْده سَوا وبُكْرة هنْكون فين؟

في الدُّنْيا في الدُّنْيا

المطرب: ياللي بتسْأل عَن الحَياة خُدْها كدَه زَي ما هيّ

فيها ابْتِسامة وفيها آه فيها أَسيَّة وحنّيَّة

الكورس: ياما الحَياة فيها اللي بيشْكيها

المطرب: واللي بيرْضيها

الكورس: آه

المطرب: واللي يقاسيها
الكورس: آه
الدُّنيا ريشة في هَوا، طايرة بغير جِناحين
إحْنا النّهارْده سَوا وبُكْرة هَنْكون فين؟
في الدُّنيا في الدُّنيا

المفردات

world	دُنْيا
feather	ريشة ج. ريشات، ريش
air	هَوا
flying	طايِر ج. طايْرين
without	بغير، من غير
wing	جْناح ج. أَجْنِحة
together	سَوا
to be	كان، يُكون
how often!	ياما
people	ناس
to meet	اتْقابِل، يِتْقابِل
appointment	مَعاد
to gather, bring together	جَمَع، يِجْمَع
to beg, plead	اتْحايِل، يِتْحايِل
separation	فُراق
to go away, keep one's distance from	بِعِد، يِبْعِد عن
to bring together, gather, embrace	ضَمّ، يُضُمّ
to separate, be separated	اتْفَرَّق، يِتْفَرَّق
around him/it	حَواليه
reason	سَبَب ج. أَسْباب
meeting	لُقى
to ask	سَأَل، يِسْأَل
life	حَياة
to take	خَد، ياخُد

just as it/she is	كدَه زَي ما هيَّ	
smile	ابْتِسامة ج. ابْتِسامات	
grief, sorrow, distress	أَسِيَّة	
affection	حنِّيَة	
to complain	شَكى، يِشْكي	
to be satisfied, content	رِضي، يِرْضى	
to suffer, endure	قاسى، يِقاسي	

ملاحظات

١- طايرة بغير جناحين

Flying without wings

(طايرة) is the active participle of (طار) so here it means "flying."

٢- ياما ناس بتتقابل

How often people meet

(ياما) is an adverb that means "much," "many times," or as here, "how often."

٣- اللي بيرضيها

What satisfies her

This expression should be (اللي بيرضـى بيها) but the poet has contracted it to make it rhyme with (بيشـكيها).

التّدريبات

١.   حطّ علامة صحَّ أو غلط قدّام الجمل دي.

أ- الدّنيا ريشة في هوا طايرة بجناحين.   ( )

ب- فيه ناس كتير بتتقابل من غير معاد.   ( )

ت- الحياة في الأغنية صعبة على طول.   ( )

ث- النّاس اللي بيتقابلوا أكيد هيفضلوا مع بعض على طول.   ( )

ج- الشّاعر مش عارف ليه الناس بتتقابل وبتتفرق.   ( )

٢. كمّل الجمل دي بكلمات من عندك.

أ- الحمامة وقفت على سور البلكونة و.............. وقعت من جسمها.

ب- الطّيارة ليها .... زي الطّيور.

ت- النّهارده عندي .... مهم السّاعة تلاتة في وسط البلد.

ث- الشّمس بتدور والأرض بتدور بتدور ....

ج- عايز نروح السّينما .... ولا عايز تشوف الفيلم لوحدك؟

٣. اختار الكلمة الصّحيحة من بين الأقواس.

أ- أحزن لحظة بين حبيبين سابوا بعض لحظة .... (الدّنيا - الحياة - الفراق)

ب- الصّدفة هي إنك تقابل حد .... (من غير معاد - من غير - معاد)

ت- وأنا صغيّر كنت باحبّ .... صور أعلام البلاد. (أجمع - ألعب - أتحايل)

ث- أحسن حاجة إنك تقبل حبيبتك .... (حنيّة - أسيّة - كده زي ما هيّ)

ج- ليه النّاس بتتقابل وبعد كده ....؟ (بتضم - بتتفرّق - بتجمع)

ح- .... يا ولاد الأكل ده كله. (واكلين - كُلوا - كَلوا)

خ- .... الواجب ده دلوقتي في الفصل. (كتبوا - اكتبوا - يكتبوا)

د- .... الشبّاك لو سمحت يا مجدي. (يفتح - افتحي - افتح)

ذ- .... الفيلم ده و.............. رأيك. (شايف، قايل - شوف، قول - تشوف، تقول)

ر- .... الكتاب من الشّنطة. (طلّعي - اطلعي - طالعة)

٤. وصّل الكلمة بعكسها.

فراق	لقى
قرب	فرَق
اتقابل	قسوة
حنية	بعد
ضمّ	افترق

٥. حطّ الكلمات دي في جمل من عندك:

دنيا - حياة - فراق - طايرة - سوا - ابتسامة - جناح

....

....

....

....

....

....

....

٦. استخرج من النص:

فعل في المستقبل

....

فعل أمر

....

اسم فاعل

....

٥ أفعال مضرعة مع (ب)

....

....

....

....

....

٣ أفعال مضارعة من غير (ب)

....

....

....

فعلين ماضيين

....

....

....
....
....

١٠

شخبط شخابيط

٢٠٠٧

كلمات: عوض بدوي - ألحان: وليد سعد - غناء: نانسي عجرم

This is a popular children's song, in which the singer warns children not to draw or paint on walls. It was presented in an album named after this song and was released in 2007. Nancy Ajram has always wanted to dedicate one of her works to children. The album, and its accompanying music video, was an important step in her career and made her extremely popular in the Arab world. The album included other children's songs, such as "Katkouta," "Shater," and "Eid Milad." As you see in this song, most Arabic children's songs are didactic and include direct advice. The children might not be affected by such directness, however, and readily grasp and apply the songs' values.

شخَبْط شخابيط لخَبْط لخابيط مسك الألوان ورَسَم ع الحيط
أعْمِل إيه وَيّاك يا حَمادة؟ اللي عَمِلْته ده أسْوأ عادة
عايز ترْسِم ارْسِم لَكِن من غير ما تْشخْبط ع الحيط
شخَبْط شخابيط لخَبْط لخابيط مسك الألوان ورَسَم ع الحيط
ارْسِم شجَرة ونيل وبُحور لَكِن ارْسِم ع السَّبورة
بُكرة تكون فَنان مَشْهور عايْزين ناخُد جنْبَك صورة
واحْلَم تكْبَر تبْقى بيكاسو، كان يُوم طِفْل وكان من نفْسُه
لَكِن ولا شخْبَط ع الحيط
شخَبْط شخابيط لخَبْط لخابيط مسك الألوان ورَسَم ع الحيط
ارْسِم واحْلَم بالمُسْتَقْبِل واللي بيحْلَم بُكرة ينول
واللي جاي ف عُمْرَك أجْمَل كُل هِواية وليها أُصول

امْسِك قَلَمَك لونَك ريشْتَك وإرْسِم بيهُم بَس ف لوحْتَك
ترْسِم ليه باللونْ ع الحيط؟
شَخْبَط شخابيط لخْبَط لخابيط مِسِك الألوان ورَسِم ع الحيط

المفردات

to scribble	شَخْبَط، يشَخْبَط	
scribble	شَخْبَطة ج. شخابيط	
to mix up, mess up	لخْبَط، يلَخْبَط	
mess, mix up	لخْبَطة ج. لخابيط	
to hold	مسِك، يمْسِك	
color	لون ج. ألْوان	
to draw	رَسَم، يرْسِم	
wall	حيط ج. حيطان	
to make, do	عَمَل، يعْمِل	
with you	وَيّاك	
worse, worst	أسْوَء	
habit	عادة ج. عادات	
to want	عايِز ج. عايْزين	
but	لكن	
without + verb	من غير ما + فعل	
tree	شَجَرة ج. شَجَر، شجرات، أشجار	
the Nile	نيل = النيل	
blackboard	سَبّورة ج. سَبّورات	
tomorrow	بُكْرة	
artist	فَنّان ج. فَنّانين	
famous	مَشْهور ج. مَشْهورين، مَشاهير	
picture	صورة ج. صوَر	
to dream	حلِم، يحْلَم	
to grow up or old, to get bigger	كبِر، يكْبَر	
to be, become	بَقى، يبْقى	
child	طِفْل ج. أطْفال	
as you wish	من نفْسه	

future	مُسْتَقْبَل
to get, gain	نال، يُنول
coming	جاي ج. جايين
age	عُمْر ج. أَعْمار
more beautiful, the most beautiful	أَجْمَل
every	كُل
hobby	هُواية ج. هُوايات
conditions, rules	أُصول
pen	قَلَم ج. إقْلام
paintbrush (or feather)	ريشة
canvas	لوحة ج. لوحات، لُوَح

ملاحظات

١- شخبط شخابيط لخبط لخابيط

Scribble, scribbles, mess, messes
(شخبط) and (لخبط) are verbs with four-letter roots.

٢- بكرة تكون فنان مشهور

May you become a famous artist (tomorrow)
Here, the present tense (تكون) is used because the phrase expresses a wish for the future. Had the poet used the future tense instead, it would have meant "tomorrow, you will be a famous artist." Thus, the choice of verb tense affects the meaning of the sentence.

٣- اللي بيحلم بكرة ينول

May he who dreams have his realized (tomorrow)
Again, here the present tense (ينول) expresses a wish—"may the dreams of dreamers come true tomorrow."

٤- ترسم ليه باللون ع الحيط؟

Here, the present tense without (ترسم) (ب) is used because it refers to the general idea of drawing on a wall, not to a real-life act of drawing. In other words, it could be translated as "why would you draw on the wall?" rather than "why are you drawing on the wall?"

التّدريبات

١. حطّ علامة صحّ أو غلط قدّام الجمل دي.

أ- حمادة مسك الألوان ورسم على الغيط.   (   )

ب- بيكاسّو رسّام مشهور.   (   )

ت- حمادة بيحبّ يرسم في اللوحة.   (   )

ث- الرّسم على السّبورة غلط.   (   )

ج- كل هواية ليها قواعد.   (   )

٢. كمّل الجمل دي بكلمات من عندك.

أ- أكتر .... باحبه الأحمر.

ب- شارلي شابلن .... مشهور.

ت- النّهارده ركبنا فلوكة في .... وكانت رحلة جميلة جدًا.

ث- بتحلم تكون إيه لمّا ....؟

ج- المدرّس ده بيكتب على .... بخطّ صغير قوي.

٣. اختار الإجابة الصحيحة من بين الأقواس.

أ- ممنوع .... في الورقة دي.   (تشخبط – تحلم – تمسك)

ب- لما اتعلمت عربي وتركي في نفس الوقت .... الاتنين ببعض.   (شخبطت – لخبطت – خططت)

ت- عايز .... إيه لما تكبر؟   (ترسم – تبقى – تاخد)

ث- عايزين .... صورة جنب أبو الهول.   (ناخد – ناكل – نحلم)

ج- الدّول المتقدمة بتخطّط .... كويس.   (للألوان – للمستقبل – للحيط)

٤. حط الكلمات دي في جمل من عندك:

بقى – عمر – هواية – لوحة – ألوان – شخبط – لخبط

٥. استخرج من النص:

٥ أفعال ماضية

....
....
....
....

٦ أفعال مضارعة

....
....
....
....
....
....

فعلين أمر

....
....

صفة على وزن أفعل

....

اسم فاعل

....

٦.   اوصف الصَورة دي.

....
....
....
....
....

من سحر عيونك

٢٠١١

كلمات: مأمون الشناوي - ألحان: محمد عبد الوهاب - غناء: ريما خشيش

This romantic poem was originally performed by Lebanese singer Sabah (who died in 2014) in the 1957 movie "إغراء" (Seduction). She starred in this film, alongside Shukri Sarhan, and it was written by Mohammed Mustafa Sami, produced by Mohamed Abdel Wahab and Barakat, and directed by Hassan al-Imam.

The version below is a cover by the Lebanese singer Rima Khcheich and it was the title track in her 2011 album "من سحر عيونك" (The magic of your eyes). The album is a live recording from a concert at the American University of Beirut that celebrated Sabah's seventy-year long singing and acting career. In the album, Khcheich performed eleven of Sabah's songs, all of which featured in her films, both in Lebanese and Egyptian Arabic, remaining as faithful as possible to the original songs.

مِن سِحُر عُيونَك ياه مِن رِمْش جْفونَك ياه
نِسيت لَيالي نَوَّرْتَهالي نِسيت ياه
أَيَام أَيَام الحنُية وِسْنين وَأَيَام تقْسى عَليَا
ساعات تكون خالي وِناسي
وِساعات حَنون وساعات قاسي
ماعُرَفْش مالك
خُد مِن جَمالك
وإدِّي خِصالك
تحْلو أكْتَر والحُبّ يكْبَر بيني وِبينك

مِن سِحْر عُيونَك ياه مِن رِمْش جُفونَك ياه
نِسيت لَيالي نَوَّرْتْهالي نسيت ياه
القُرْب تِنْسى جَمال لَياليه والوَرْد لِسّه عَبيرَك فيه
بِدْموع عينيَا فِضلَت أَرْويه وأَخَلّي نار شوقي تِدَفَّيه
طَوَّلْت بُعْدَك
وأَنا وَحدي بَعْدَك
يا تَرى إنْتَ وَحْدَك
تَعالى عَنْدي ناخُد وندّي بيني وبينَك
مِن سِحْر عُيونَك ياه مِن رِمْش جُفونَك ياه
نِسيت لَيالي نَوَّرْتْهالي نسيت ياه

المفردات

magic, charm	سحر
eye	عين ج. عيون (مؤنثة)
Oh my God! Wow!	ياه
eyelash	رمش ج. رموش
eyelid	جفن ج. جفون
to forget	نسي، ينسى
night	ليلة ج. ليالي
to light	نور، ينور
day	يوم ج. أيام
year	سنة ج. سنين
carefree	خالي/ة
severe, harsh, cruel	قاسي/ة
to know	عرف، يعرف
what's wrong with you?	مالك؟
to take	خد، ياخد
beauty	جمال
to give	إدى، يدي
characteristic	خصلة ج. خصال
to become beautiful/handsome	احلو، يحلو
many	كتير/ة ج. كتار
love	حب

between	بين . . . وبين . . .	
closeness, togetherness	قرب	
rose	وردة ج. وردات/ورد/ورود	
still	لسه	
fragrance	عبير	
tear	دمعة ج. دمعات/دمع/دموع	
to keep	فضل، يفضل	
to water	روى، يروي	
to make, let	خلى، يخلي	
fire	نار ج. نيران	
longing	شوق ج. أشواق	
to warm	دفى، يدفي	
to extend, elongate	طول، يطول	
alone (for the first-person, singular prounoun)	وحدي	
I wonder	يا ترى	
Come!	تعالى	

ملاحظات

١- من سحر عيونك ياه

The magic of your eyes - oh my!
(ياه) is a word used to express astonishment or surprise.

٢- تعالى عندي ناخد وندي

(تعالى) is the imperative form of (جه، ييجي). The feminine form is (تعالي) and the plural is (تعالوا).

التدريبات

١.   حط علامة صح أو غلط قدام الجمل دي.
أ- الأغنية أصلاً بتاعة ريما خشيش.   (   )

ب- الشاعر عايز حبيبته تبعد عنه.   (   )

ت- حبيبة الشاعر غريبة وموودية.   (   )

ث- الشاعر بكى عشان حبيبته بعيدة عنه.   (   )

ج- الشاعر قاعد لوحده.   (   )

٢. كمل الجمل دي بكلمات من عندك.

أ- أنا .... بنام الساعة ١٢، و.................. بنام بدري الساعة ١٠ مثلًا.

ب- يا .... فاطمة بتبكي ليه؟

ت- ممكن .... الأوضة لو سمحت، دي ضلمة خالص.

ث- معظم العلماء مش بيؤمنوا بالـ..................

ج- فيه شعرة من .... دخلت في عيني.

٣. اختار الكلمة الصحيحة من بين الأقواس.

أ- .... اللبن باظ عشان سيبته بره التلاجة!   (رمش – ياه – جفن)

ب- أنا ماعملتش الواجب عشان كنت ....   (ناسي – قاسي – حنون)

ت- مش ممكن أنزل من البيت قبل ما .... الزرع.   (أنور – أحلو – أروي)

ث- إنتي .... تلعبي من الصبح وما ذاكرتيش ولا ساعة واحدة.   (فضلتي – خليتي – عرفتي)

ج- إنت .... قوي في صالة البلاي ستيشان، استنيتك كتير.   (وحدك – طولت – نسيت)

٤. استخرج من النص:

٩ أفعال مضارعة – ٤ أفعال ماضية – ٣ أفعال أمر – فعل منفي

٥. حط الكلمات دي في جمل من عندك:

يكبر – ينور – سحر – رموش – دموع – فضل – خلى

٦. وصل الكلمة بعكسها.

حنية	ناسي
فاكر	قسوة
خد	حنون
قاسي	يصغر
يكبر	هات

....
....
....
....
....

١٢

حاضر يا زهر

٢٠٠٥

كلمات: عبد الرحيم منصور - ألحان: هاني شنودة - غناء: محمد منير

The song addresses dice, a symbol of luck and chance. The singer accuses the dice of being fickle and of playing games with people, making them happy only to subsequently make them cry, and deserting them only to befriend them once again.

حاضر يا زَهْر! نَعَمين يا زَهْر!

عاجُبَك كده لِعْبَك يا زَهْر؟

نِسْهَر سَوا، نِلْعَب سَوا

تِفْرحْنا يوم ونبكي شَهْر

تخاصِمْنا يوم، تصالِحْنا شَهْر

عاجبك يا زَهْر؟ أَمْرَك يا زَهْر!

عامل حَمَل وإنْتَ غول

أَبْقى الجَمَل وإنْتَ الحُمول

ارْمي البَياض أو بَس قول

ولا عَشان أنا عَنْدي صَبْر

أَمْرَك يا زَهْر! حاضر يا زَهْر!

يا أبو أَلْف وِش وأَلْف عين

وأَلْف ضِحْكة ملوّنين

وراك وراك واخدْني فين؟

إنْتَ دَلال ولا إنْتَ أَمْر؟

أَمْرَك يا زَهْر! حاضر يا زَهْر!

٦٥   20 Egyptian Songs

المفردات

fine	حاضِر
dice	زَهْر
to please	عَجَب، يِعْجِب
like this, in this way	كده
playing	لِعْب
together	سَوا
to make (someone) happy	فَرَّح، يِفَرَّح / يِفْرِح(بِـ)
to cry, weep	بَكى، يِبْكي
month	شَهْر ج. شُهور
to break up with, to argue or fight with	خاصِم، يِخاصِم
to make up with	صالِح، يِصالِح
order, command	أَمْر ج. أَوامِر
to make, do	عَمَل، يِعْمِل
lamb	حَمَل ج. حِمْلان
camel	جَمَل ج. جِمال
burden	حِمْل ج. حُمول
to throw	رَمى، يِرْمي
the whiteness	البَياض
just	بَس
to say	قال، يُقول
or	وَلّا
patience	صَبْر
thousand	أَلْف
face	وِشّ ج. وُشوش
laugh	ضِحْكة
colorful, changeable	مِلَوِّن ج. مِلَوِّنين
behind (opposite: in front of)	ورا (العكس: قُدّام)
to take	خَد ج. ياخُد
lighthearted teasing	دَلال

ملاحظات

١- نعمين يا زهر

Oh yes, dice!
(نعمين) is the dual of the word (نعم), meaning "yes." Here it adds emphasis.

٢- تفرحنا يوم ونبكي شهر

Make us happy for a day, and cry for a month
These verbs are used without (بـ) as they are not referring to concrete events but to abstract ideas.

٣- عامل حمل وإنت غول

Make out you are a lamb, when really you're a ghoul
(عامل) is the active participle of (عمل), and here has the meaning of "to pretend."
(غول) means ghoul, an imaginary creature that can take different shapes and that appears in uninhabited areas, especially deserts and graveyards. The ghoul is mentioned in many tales, including *The Thousand and One Nights*. In this song, "ghoul" is used to symbolize cruelty and the lack of mercy.

٤- أبقى الجمل وإنت الحمول

Be the camel, even though you're the camel
Again, the present tense verb (إبقى) is used without (بـ) as it does not refer to a real-life instance of staying but rather to the abstract idea of it.

٥- ارمي البياض

Get your fortune told
In some Bedouin communities, casting pebbles is used as a means of fortune-telling and divination. Specifically, *bayad* refers to the payment made to the diviner before the divination occurs; it comes from *abyad* (white) as it is believed that the fee whitens the heart of the diviner, ensuring their

sincerity in revealing the future. In the context of the song, the singer asks luck (or the figure of the dice) to reveal their fortune.

٦- يا أبو ألف وش وألف عين

O he who has a thousand faces and a thousand eyes
(أبو) here means "he who has." The singer characterizes the dice to have a thousand faces (ألف وش) and a thousand eyes (ألف عين), proposing the idea that luck is fickle and constantly changing.

٧- وراك وراك واخدني فين

Everywhere you go, where to go
(وراك وراك) means, literally, "behind you behind you," and has the meaning of being followed everywhere.

٨- إنت دلال ولا إنت أمر

Are you luck or are these orders?
In this expression, the poet asks luck if it is just teasing them or whether it is actually ordering them around and controlling their life.
(وَلّا) means "or," whereas the English might read "either . . . or."

التّدريبات

١.   حطّ علامة صحّ أو غلط قدام الجمل دي.

أ- الحظّ بيفرحنا يوم ويزعّلنا شهر.   (   )

ب- الحظّ زي الغول.   (   )

ت- الحظّ بيخاصمنا شهر وبيصالحنا يوم.   (   )

ث- الحظّ بألف وشّ وألف عين.   (   )

ج- الشّاعر هيمشي قدّام الحظّ.   (   )

٢.   كمّل الجمل دي بكلمات من عندك.

أ- رحت الهرم وركبت .... هناك بس كان عالي قوي.

ب- إمبارح .... جامد، مانمتش إلّا السّاعة أربعة الفجر.

ت- ليه .... صاحبك وإنت عارف إنه بيحبك؟

ث- مش باقدر أشوف طفل .... وأفضل ساكت ماعملش حاجة.

ج- حاضر، .... يا ماما، هاعمل كل اللي إنتي عايزاه.

٣. اختار الكلمة الصحيحة من بين الأقواس.

أ- .... الطاولة ضاع، لازم نشتري واحد جديد. (غول – زهر – صبر)

ب- .... هو الخروف الصغير. (الحمل – الجمل – الغول)

ت- بنتي .... صاحبتها، كانت مخاصماها من شهر. (صالحت – سهرت – نعمين)

ث- رسمت عشر لوحات، تلاتة أبيض وإسود و سبعة .... (عينين – بياض – ملونين)

ج- فيلم شارلي شابلن الأخير .... قوي. (عاجبني – واخدني – خاصمني)

٤. حطَّ الكلمات دي في جمل من عندك:

صبر – حَمَل – خاصم – صالح – ضحكة – زهر

....
....
....
....
....
....
....

٥. استخرج من النص:

٤ أسماء فاعل

....
....
....
....

٦ أفعال مضارعة

....
....
....
....
....
....

فعلي أمر

....
....

٦.   اوصف الصَّورة دي.

....

....

....

....

١٣

ماما يا حلوة

(الستينات)

كلمات: كمال منصور – ألحان: منير مراد – غناء: شادية

This sentimental song is addressed to the poet's mother. It is one of the most popular Mother's Day songs in Egypt and is played on the radio every year on March 21, the day on which Mother's Day is celebrated in Egypt.

ماما يا حلْوة يا أَجْمَل غِنْوة
عايْشة في قَلْبي وجُوَّه كَياني
غالْية عليَّا وضَيّ عينيَّا
يا أَوِّل كِلْمة نَطَقْها لْساني
ماما ماما ماما يا ماما
إنْتي يا ماما مَلاك م الجَنّة
تَحْت جناحك أَعيش وأَتْهَنَّى
إنْتي حَياتي وابْتِساماتي
إنْتي مُنايا وكُلّ هَنايا
مين رَبَّاني مين ومين هَنّاني مين
غيرك إنْتي يا حلْوة يا ماما؟
ماما ماما ماما يا ماما
لَمّا أَضُمّك وتْضُميني
تِبْقى الدُنْيا مُش سايْعاني
ويزيد شوقي وأَلْقى حَنيني
بيخَلّيني أَضُمّك تاني
مين رَبَّاني مين ومين هَنّاني مين
غيرك إنْتي يا حلْوة يا ماما؟

ماما ماما ماما يا ماما

مَهْما أَلَفّ الدُّنيا يوماتي

مالْقاش زَيُّكْ فـ الدُّنيا دي

أَسْعَد لَحْظة في كُلّ حَياتي

لَمّا ألاقيكي يا ماما قُصادي

مين رَبّاني مين ومين هَنّاني مين

غيرك إِنْتي يا حلْوة يا ماما؟

ماما ماما ماما يا ماما

المفردات

sweet	حِلْو ج. حلْوين
song	غنْوة
to live	عاش، يعيش
heart	قَلْب ج. قُلوب
inside (opposite: outside)	جُوَّه (العكس: بَرَّه)
being, existence	كَيان
dear	غالي ج. غاليين
light	ضَي
first	أَوِّل
word	كلْمة ج. كلْمات
to pronounce, speak	نَطَق، يِنْطَق
tongue	لسان ج. أَلْسنة
angel	مَلاك ج. مَلايْكة
paradise, heaven	جَنّة ج. جَنّات
under (opposite: above)	تَحْت (العكس: فوق)
wing	جْناح ج. أَجْنحة
to enjoy, be delighted, take plea-sure	اتْهَنَى، يِتْهَنَى
life	حَياة
smile	ابْتِسامة ج. ابْتِسامات
wish	مُنى
happiness, joy	هَنا
to raise, bring up	رَبَّى، يِربِّي

else, except	غير
to increase	زاد، يِزيد
longing	شوق ج. أَشْواق
to find	لَقى، يِلْقى
yearning	حَنين
to make	خَلَّى، يِخَلِّي
again	تاني
even if	مَهْما
to go around	لَفَّ، يِلِفّ
everyday	يوماتي
to find	لاقى، يِلاقي
in front of (opposite: behind)	قُصاد (العكس: وَرا)
moment	لَحْظة ج. لَحْظات

ملاحظات

١- تحت جناحك أعيش وأتهنَّى

Under your wing, I would live and rejoice
The verbs use the present tense without (بـ) to indicate a hypothetical situation (I would live and rejoice) rather than something that actually takes
place (I live and rejoice).

٢- لما أضمّك وتضمّيني تبقى الدّنيا مش سايعاني

When I hold you and you hold me, the world cannot contain me
Unlike the example above, here the verbs are used without (بـ) for the sake
of the poem's rhythm, but there is no grammatical reason for this. (سايعاني)
is formed from the active participle (سايعة), in its feminine form to agree
with (الدّنيا), and the first-person suffix (ني). When you add a suffix to the
feminine form of the active participle (اسم الفاعل), the letter (ة) changes into
(ا). For example:
She has eaten it.

واكلة – واكلاه

She wants you.

عايزة ___ عايزاك

She understands us.

فاهمة ___ فاهمانا

التّدريبات

١. حطّ علامة صحّ وغلط قدّام الجمل دي.

أ- الأَمّ هي أحلى غنوة. ( )

ب- أول كلمة بينطقها الطّفل "ماما." ( )

ت- الأَمّ بتربّي الطفل لوحدها. ( )

ث- ضَمّ يعني حَضَن. ( )

٢. كمّل الجمل دي بكلمات من عندك.

أ- أول اسم نطقه .... كان اسم أختي فيفي.

ب- الطير عنده .... بيطير بيهم.

ت- لما نجحت وخلصت الجامعة كانت الدنيا مش ....

ث- أسعد .... في حياتي كانت لما بُست حبيبتي لأول مرة.

ج- الراجل بتاع الفول بيعدّي من شارعنا .... حتى الجمعة والسبت.

٣. اختار الإجابة الصحيحة من بين الأقواس.

أ- .... درست عربي في مراكز مش هتتعلمه إلا لما تمارسه. (مهما - نطق - تبقى)

ب- أمي مش ست عادية، دي .... من الجنة. (إنسان - أم - ملاك)

ت- بعد ما أبويا وأمي ماتوا جدي اللي .... (سايعاني - ربّاني - هنّاني)

ث- تفتكر كل الأجانب ممكن .... كل حروف العربي؟ (يزيدوا - ينطقوا - يبقوا)

ج- مش هاكون مبسوط يا ماما إلا لما .... قصاد عيني. (أضمك - ألاقيكي - منايا)

ح- إيه .... فيلم شفته في السّينما؟ (جميل - جمال - أجمل)

٤. صحّح الكلمة اللي تحتها خط في الجمل دي.

أ- روسيا كبير بلد في آسيا.

ب- الجامع الأزهر قديم ولا مسجد الحسين؟

ت- البنت اللي حبيتها كانت جميلة واحدة فيهم.

ث- السكر أغلى على الرز.

ج- أنا مهتم أجمل منك باللغات.

٥. حطّ الكلمات دي في جمل من عندك:

نطق - لسان - جناح - ربّى - غالي - لقى

٦. استخرج من النص:
صفة على وزن أفعل

....

....

اسمي فاعل

....

....

١٠ أفعال مضارعة

....

....

....

....

....

....

....

....

فعلين ماضيين

....

....

....
....
....
....
....

١٤

فين الحقيقة؟

١٩٩٩

كلمات: عبد الرحيم منصور – ألحان: عبد العظيم عويضة – غناء: محمد منير

This song, written by Abdel Rihim Mansur, was originally recorded by Mohamed Mounir in 1976, and appeared in the opening sequence of the TV series "اللسان المرّ" (The Sour Tongue). It was then recorded again by Mounir in 1999 with a different arrangement and a faster tempo. In the song, Mansur talks about how the truth constantly changes, like the sunrise and the sunset, making it hard to catch. He goes on to speak about different kinds of people, especially those whose tongues are sour but hearts are pure, adding that they tell the truth even if it's painful. The singer pronounces the letter (ق) as (g) in the word (gram) according to the Upper Egypt dialect, which the characters use in the TV series mentioned earlier.

فين الحقيقة يا خال؟ تعْبت علَشانها القُلوب
في كلَّ لَحْظة بحال زيّ الشُروق والغُروب
وإيه ف القُلوب يا خال؟ قلوب ماليها السُّؤال
قُلوب قلوب خاوْية لا فيها خير ولا شَر
وقلوب قلوب غاوْية تجرَح كتير وتضُر
وأبو القليب صافي دافي ولسانه مُرّ
مُرّ السُؤال يا خال للّي تعْبوا ف الدُروب
طَب نعْمل إيه أُمَال؟ نفْتَح بيبان القُلوب
أَمْرَك غريب يا خال تفْتَح بيبان الخَيال
قُلوب قُلوب شارْدة تعْرَفْش إيه السَّر
فارْدة الجناح فارْدة تبْحَثْلها على بَر
وأبو القليب صافي دافي ولسانه مُرّ

truth	حَقيقة ج. حَقايِق
(maternal) uncle	خال ج. خِلان
to get tired	تِعِب، يِتْعب
for, because of	عَلَشان
in a case of, in a state	بِحال
changing every moment	في كُل لَحْظة بِحال
as, like	زَي
sunrise	شُروق
sunset	غُروب
to fill	مَلى، يِمْلى
question	سُؤال ج. أَسْئِلة
empty	خاوي
neither . . . nor	لا . . . ولا
goodness	خير
evil	شر
keen, eager for	غاوي ج. غاوْيين
wound	جَرْح ج. جُروح
many, much	كتير ج. كُتار
to harm, injure	ضَرّ، يُضُرّ
little heart (the diminutive of heart)	قلِيب
pure	صافي ج. صافْيِين
warm	دافي ج. دافْيِين
tongue	لِسان ج. أَلْسِنة
bitter	مُرَ
for those who	للي
path, way	دَرْب ج. دُروب
OK, so	طَب
to do	عَمَل، يِعْمِل
to open	فَتَح، يِفْتَح

door	باب ج. بِيبان	
attitude, state, situation	أَمْر ج. أُمور	
strange, amazing	غريب ج. غُراب	
imagination	خَيال	
absentminded, preoccupied, inattentive	شارِد ج. شارْدين	
to know	عرف، يِعرَف	
secret	سِرّ ج. أَسْرار	
stretching	فارِد ج. فارْدين	
wing	جَناح ج. أَجْنِحة	
to search	بَحَث، يِبْحَث	
land	بَرَ	

ملاحظات

١- فين الحقيقة يا خال

What's the truth, Uncle?
In certain (often rural) dialects, (خال) is used to refer respectfully to older men, even if they are unrelated to the speaker.

٢- طب نعمل إيه أمال؟ نفتح بيبان القلوب

So what do we do, I wonder? Do we open the hearts' doors?
(أمال) is used in questions to add emphasis and/or express confusion. It is similar to the English phrase "I wonder," or empathetic words such as "so," or "then."
For example:
I wonder why you didn't take any medication until now?

أمال ليه ماخدتش دوا لحد دلوقتي؟

Why did you leave Egypt, then, if you love it so much?

أمال إنت سبت مصر ليه إذا كنت بتحبها؟

So where are you from and where did you learn English?

أمال إنت منين أصلًا واتعلمت إنجليزي فين؟

٣- قلوب شاردة تعرفش إيه السر

Wandering hearts know/have no secrets
(تعرفش) is an abbreviation of (ماتعرفش): it/she doesn't know.

التّدريبات

١. حطّ علامة صح أو غلط قدّام الجمل دي.

أ- القلوب تعبت عشان بتدوّر على الحقيقة.   (   )

ب- فيه قلوب لا فيها خير ولا شرّ.   (   )

ت- الشّخصيّة اللي بتكلّم الكورس (chorus) خيالها ضيّق.   (   )

ث- اللي قلبه صافي لسانه مرّ.   (   )

ج- إحنا عارفين ليه فيه قلوب شاردة.   (   )

٢. كمّل الجمل دي بكلمات من عندك.

أ- باحب أنزل البحر في مطروح عشان المَيَّة هناك ....

ب- نادرًا إن القمر يطلع بين .... و................ الشمس، غالبًا بنشوفه بالليل بس.

ت- فيه ناس كتير مابيجيش منهم لا .... ولا ....، موجودين كإنهم مش موجودين.

ث- الحرب بين البلدين كانت في .... ولّا في البحر؟

ج- النّهارده الامتحان كان مية .... في النّحو بس.

٣. اختار الكلمة الصحيحة من بين الأقواس.

أ- بنتي .... تتفرج على التلفزيون بالليل.   (صافية - غاوية - خاوية)

ب- بص الصقر بيطير وهو .... جناحه إزاي.   (فارد - شارد - صافي)

ت- الأوضة دي التراب ....، عايزة تنضيف طول اليوم.   (دافيها - ماليها - غاويها)

ث- اللي بيحرك الأحداث في الحكاية الشّعبيّة هو .... بس.   (الخيال - الدروب - المرّ)

ج- الولد .... إيده وهو بيلعب بالسّكينة.   (ضرّ - تعب - جرح)

٤. وصّل الكلمة بعكسها.

خير   غُروب

جَرَح   شَرّ

شُروق   نَفَع

ضَرّ   فَرد

طَوى   داوى

٥.   حطَّ الكلمات دي في جمل من عندك:

صافي ‑ خيال ‑ سِرّ ‑ بَرَ ‑ مُرَ ‑ شَرَ

....

....

....

....

....

....

٦.   استخرج من النص:

٦ أسماء فاعل

....

....

....

....

....

....

٣ أفعال مضارعة

....

....

....

فعل ماضي

....

....
....
....
....
....

١٥

سالمة يا سلامة

١٩٧٧

كلمات: صلاح جاهين - ألحان: جيف برنيف - غناء: داليدا

Like many of Dalida's songs, this one deals with homesickness, a topic she was no stranger to, having spent much of her life living away from her homeland, Egypt.

The refrain "سالمة يا سلامة" which figuratively means "go safely," because "سالمة" means "safe," was taken from the popular folk song of the same name, originally recorded by Sayed Darwish in 1919. The refrain became a common expression in Egypt and can be seen painted on boats or heard sung by people on trips.

ف الدُنيا الكبيرة وبلادُها الكتيرة
لَفَيت لفَيت لفَيت
ولَمّا ناداني حُبّي الأوّلاني
سِبْت كُلّه وجيت وجيت
وفي حُضْنه اتْرميت وغَنّيت
سالْمة يا سَلامة رُحْنا وجينا بالسَّلامة
لِسّه الحُبّ صافي ولِسّه الجو دافي
ولِسّه فيه قَمَر
ويبعد الغارب نِتْلَمْلِم في قارب
ويطول السَّهَر السَّهَر
والسَّمَر والغِنى كُلّنا
سالْمة يا سَلامة رُحْنا وجينا بالسَّلامة
فيه شَجَرة جُوّه جنينة عَليها عَلامة

أَنا ياما كُنْت بافَكَّر فيها
وباسْأَل ياما يا تَرى مَوْجودة؟
وقَلْبي مَحْفوظ فيها؟
أَيوه مَوْجودة وقَلْبي مَحْفوظ فيها
سالْمة يا سَلامة رُحْنا وجينا بالسَّلامة
ف الدُّنيا الكَبيرة وبلادْها الكَتيرة
لَفَّيت لَفَّيت لَفَّيت
ولَمّا ناداني حُبّي الأَوَّلاني
سِبْت كُلّه وجيت وجيت
وفي حُضْنه اتْرَميت وغَنَّيت
سالْمة يا سَلامة رُحْنا وجينا بالسَّلامة

المفردات

country	بَلَد ج. بلاد
first	أَوَّلاني
to let, leave	ساب، يِسيب
everything	كُلّه
to come	جه، يِيجي
embrace, hug	حَضَن، يُحْضُن
safe	سالِم ج. سالْمين
safety	سَلامة
still	لِسّه
there is/are	فيه
sunset	مَغْرِب ج. مَغارِب
to get together	اتْلَمْلِم، يِتْلَمْلِم
boat	قارِب ج. قَوارِب
to be long, extend	طال، يُطول
chatting at night or in the evening	سَمَر
singing	غُنى
together, all of us	كُلّنا
garden	جنينة ج. جَناين
sign, mark	عَلامة ج. عَلامات
to think about	فَكَّر، يِفَكَّر في

to ask	سَأَل، يِسْأَل	
I wonder	يا تَرَى	
existing, present	مَوْجود ج. مَوْجودين	
preserved	مَحْفوظ ج. مَحْفوظين	

ملاحظات

١- وفـي حُضْنه اتْرَميت وغَنَّيت

Into his arms I threw myself, and sang

(اتْرَميت) is the passive form of the verb (رَمـى), starting with the syllable (اتـ), and, as is often the case with this form, has a passive meaning: to be thrown.

٢- ويَبعْد المَغارب نتْلَمْلِم فـي قارِب ويُطوِل السَّهَر والسَّمَر والغُنـى كُلِّنا

After sunset, we gather in a boat and stay up late, chatting and singing together

Here, the poet talks about a popular Egyptian pastime: sailing a felucca along the Nile to see the sunset and spend the night chatting and singing. Both the singular and plural forms, (المَغارب) and (المَغْرب), can be used to mean sunset. This is also true for the word afternoon, where either (العصاري) or (العصـر) can be used.

التّدريبات

١.   حطّ علامة صحّ أو غلط قدام الجمل دي.

أ- الشاعر ما رجعش بلده تاني.   (   )

ب- الجو في مصر دافي.   (   )

ت- المصريين بيركبوا مركب بعد الفجر.   (   )

ث- المصريين بيحبوا يغنوا في المراكب.   (   )

ج- المصريين بيسهروا كتير.   (   )

٢.   كمَل الجمل دي بكلمات من عندك.

أ- أول ما ماما رجعت من السَفر .... في حضنها.

ب- عشان بانام بدري ماباشوفش .... وماباستمتعش بمنظره.

ت- باحبّ الشَاي .... لا سخن ولا بارد.

ث- ماعرفتش أصحى الصبح بدري بسبب .... إمبارح.

ج- في الصَيف في مصر الجو بيبدأ يحلو شوية بعد ....

٣. اختار الكلمة الصحيحة من بين الأقواس.

أ- النَّهارده فيه حفلة .... في المدرسة هتبدأ السَّاعة ستَّة بالليل. (سهر - قمر - سمر)

ب- أنا وحبيبتي رسمنا .... على أجمل شجرة في الجنينة. (قلب - قارب - قمر)

ت- إمبارح .... كتير ومانمتش كويس. (بافكر - كنت بافكر - فكرت)

ث- الفيلم ده فيه أحداث كتير ورقص و .... (سمر - غنى - سهر)

٤. حطّ الكلمات دي في جمل من عندك:

صافي - دافي - سهر - قارب - علامة - غَنَّى

....

....

....

....

....

٥. استخرج من النص:

اسم فاعل

....

اسمي مفعول

....

....

٧ أفعال ماضية

....

....

....

....

....

....

٤ أفعال مضارعة

....

....

....

....

....
....
....
....
....

١٦

الدنيا ربيع

١٩٧٥

كلمات: صلاح جاهين - ألحان: كمال الطويل - غناء: سعاد حسني

This song is the most commonly sung during *Sham al-Nisim*, the traditional Egyptian celebration of spring that dates back to pharaonic times. It exalts signs of spring, such as the blossoming of roses, widespread joy and happiness, and the warmth that follows the winter season.

The song was performed in the film "أميرة حبي أنا" (Amira, My Love), starring Suad Hosni and Husain Fahmi, directed by Hassan al-Imam, and written by Salah Jahin, Mamdouh al-Lithy, and Hassan al-Imam. The song came to be part of the movie when Suad Hosni, by chance, encountered composer Kamal al-Tawil on her way to the set. She asked al-Tawil to write music for the film, and the song was recorded in a day.

الدُّنْيا رَبيع والجَو بَديع
قَفِّل لي عَلى كُل المَواضيع
قَفِّل قَفِّل قَفِّل قَفِّل
مافيناش كاني ومافيناش ماني
كاني ماني إيه ده الدُّنْيا رَبيع
الدُّنْيا رَبيع الدُّنْيا رَبيع
الشَّجَر الناشف بَقى وِرُور، اللَّه!
والطَّير بَقى لعَبي ومُتَهَوِّر، كده هو؟
وإحْنا هَنْفَرْفِش إمْتى أَمَال
دِلْوَقْتي وَلَّا في سِبْتَمْبِر
قال لَك قال لَك قال لَك إيه قال لَك آه

قال لَك فَرْفَشة اليوم ماتْأَجُلْهاش للغَد، الغَد الغَد
واللي هِنْظْبُطُه مَهْمومٌ راح نِزْعَل مِنُّه بجَد، بجَد بجَد
ياللا مُباراة ياللا مُسابْقة مين أشْطَر ف الضُّحْكة الرَّايْقة؟
أبو دَم خَفيف طَبْعًا يِكْسَب وأبو دَم تقيل طَبْعًا لأ
الوَرْد مفَتَّح شوفوا بِيُرْقُص ويداري كسوفُه
واللي يِحبّ النُّبي يا إخْوانَ ع الواحْدة يِسَقَّف بكْفوفُه
قال لَك قال لَك قال لَك قال لَك إيه قال لَك قال لَك آه
قال لَك وَصْفة بَلَدِيّة للصِّحّة وطولة العُمْر، العُمْر العُمْر
خُدْ شَمْس وِهوا عَلى مَيّة بَلا دَوا بَلا عَيا بَلا مُرّ، بَلا مُرّ

المفردات

it's spring	الدنيا ربيع	
weather	جو	
wonderful	بديع/ة	
to close	قَفَل، يِقْفِل	
subject, topic	موضوع ج. مواضيع	
we don't bother	مافيناش	
silly or trivial chatter	كاني وماني	
dry	ناشف/ة	
youthful, vigorous	ورور	
Great! Wow!	الله!	
bird	طير ج. طيور	
playful	لعبي/ة	
reckless, rash	متهور/ة	
really?	كده هو؟	
to recover, revive	فرفش، يفرفش	
happiness, joy, rapture	فرفشة	
today	اليوم	
to postpone	أجل، يأجل	
tomorrow	الغد	
to catch	ظبط، يظبط	
concerned, worried	مهموم/ة	
will	راح	

to upset	زعل، يزعل
seriously, really	بجد
match	مباراة ج. مباريات
competition	مسابقة ج. مسابقات
clever, good	شاطر/ة
laughter	ضحكة ج. ضحكات
pure	رايق/ة
funny	أبو دم خفيف
of course	طبعًا
to win	كسب، يكسب
lacking any sense of humor, unpleasant, vile	أبو دم تقيل
to blossom	فَتَح، يِفَتَّح
to dance	رَقَص، يُرْقُص
to hide	دارى، يِداري
shyness	كُسوف
prophet	نَبي ج. أَنْبِيا، أَنْبِياء
brothers, guys	إخْوان
to clap	سَقَّف، يِسَقَّف
palm of the hand	كَفّ ج. كُفوف
prescription, recipe	وَصْفة
local	بَلَدي/ة
health	صِحّة
long life	طولة العُمْر
medicine, drug	دَوا
illness	عَيا
bitter	مُرَ

١- كاني ماني

Babble/drivel

This is an old expression that is etymologically derived from ancient Egyptian words that mean "fat" or "butter" (كاني), and "honey" (ماني). Some assert that ancient Egyptians used to solicit charity from priests by offering them these items. It can be used to express disapproval—see examples of its usage in the following:

No ifs or buts

لا كاني ولا ماني

Something or the other

كاني وماني

If you frequently fail to attend, you will be fired. I'm warning you now so you won't give me useless excuses.

لو غبت كتير هتترفد، أديني بقول لك أهو عشان ماتجيش ساعتها تقول كاني وماني.

٢- دلوقتي ولا في سبتمبر

Now or in September

The poet uses September as a symbol for the beginning of autumn, the counterpoint of spring.

٣- قال لك فرفشة اليوم ماتأجلهاش للغد

Don't put off today's joy until tomorrow

(ماتأجلهاش) is the negative imperative form of (الغد). (أجّل، يأجّل) is a modern standard Arabic word that means (tomorrow) and is equivalent to the Egyptian colloquial Arabic word (بكرة). The poet used the modern standard Arabic word for the rhyme.

٤- أبو دم خفيف

He who is light-hearted

(أبو) here means "he who has/is." (أم) can similarly be used to mean "she who has/is." Adjectives with (أبو) and (أم) are commonly used in Egyptian Arabic, such as:

The man with the glasses

الراجل أبو نضارة

The girl with the white veil

البنت أم طرحة بيضا

٥- واللي يحب النبي . . . يسقف بكفوفه

For the love of the Prophet, clap your hands
(اللي يحب النبي) literally means "those who love the Prophet" and is a common expression used to urge people to do something. For example,
For the love of the prophet, dance with us.

اللي يحب النبي يرقص معانا.

التدريبات

١. حط علامة صح أو غلط قدام الجمل دي.

أ- الشاعر عايز يتكلم في مواضيع كتير في الربيع. (   )

ب- الشجر بيكون ناشف في الربيع. (   )

ت- المفروض الناس تفرفش في سبتمبر. (   )

ث- الشاعر عايز يعمل مسابقة في الضحك. (   )

ج- أبو دم خفيف هيخسر وأبو دم تقيل هيكسب. (   )

٢. كمل الجمل دي بكلمات من عندك.

أ- النهارده هنشوف .... كرة القدم بين ريال مدريد وبرشلونة.

ب- .... طالب في الفصل جاب ٢٠ من ٢٠ في الامتحان وخد جايزة.

ت- لاعب ألماني هو اللي فاز في .... العالمية للياقة البدنية.

ث- تيجي .... في النايت كلاب (nightclub) النهارده، بقى لنا كتير ماخرجناش.

ج- أنا مش عايز أتكلم في .... ده عشان بيدايقني.

٣. اختار الكلمة الصحيحة من بين الأقواس.

أ- في مصر الجو بيكون حلو قوي في .... في أبريل. (الصيف - الربيع - الشتا)

ب- كل الناس في الجامعة بيقولوا على البنت دي إنها .... (كاني - ماني - لعبة)

ت- إنت بتقول اللاب توب (laptop) غالي، .... ليه اشتريته؟ (أمال - إمتى - فرفشة)

ث- الولد ده .... ممكن يعمل أي حاجة في أي وقت.   (دمه خفيف - دمه تقيل - متهور)

ج- .... عمل اليوم للغد.   (ماتأجلش - ماتزعلش - ماتفرفرش)

٤. وصل الكلمة بعكسها.

ناشف	تقيل
قفَل	شاطر
خايب	طري
خفيف	يكسب
يخسر	فتَح

٥. استخرج من النص:

٣ أفعال أمر

....

....

....

فعلين ماضيين

....

....

فعلين في المستقبل

....

....

٥ أفعال مضارعة

....

....

....

....

....

صفة أفعل التفضيل

....

٦. حط الكلمات دي في جمل من عندك:

ظَبَط - زعل - مهموم - وصفة - صحة - طولة العمر - يسقف

....

....

....

....

....

....

....

....

١٧

أحسن ناس

١٩٧٩

كلمات: صلاح جاهين – ألحان: سمير حبيب – غناء: داليدا

Salah Jahin wrote patriotic songs using informal and traditional Egyptian expressions and words, such as "صورة" (Picture), "بالأحضان" (With an Embrace), including the song featured here "أحسن ناس" (The Best People). In this song, Jahin praises all Egyptians from different backgrounds and communities by running through different cities in Egypt and detailing their cultural, architectural, and geographic features. Dalida was the best singer to perform this brand of nostalgia-inducing song, since she was born and raised in Egypt but lived half of her life in Europe while maintaining ties to her country of birth.

آدينا بنُدَردِش، وَرانا إيه؟ وَرانا إيه؟
بنُحَكي ونُفَرفِش، وَرانا إيه؟ وَرانا إيه؟
نِحبّ نِتْعَرَّف، وَرانا إيه؟ نحبّ نِتْشَرَّف، وَرانا إيه؟
ومُنين يا بَلدينا؟ وبَلَدَكو إيه؟
أحَسَن ناس أحَسَن ناس
سوهاج بَلَد المَواويل، سوهاج بُرج الزَغاليل
سوهاج يا حَبيبي يا حَبيبي، سوهاج دي عَروسِة النَيل
سوهاج يا بوي عالَم شَغّال يِرْخَصْلُه المال
رِجالة جَدّ وحمْل جبال يا بَلَدينا بَلَدينا
عَلى كوبْري بَنْها يا نور عيني
مَنْديل حبيبي طَرَف عيني
بَعْد الفُراق والأَشْواق جَمَع الهَوى بينُه وبيني

عَلى كوبْري بَنْها، عَلى كوبْري بَنْها
يا إسْماعيليّة يا إسْماعيليّة أَحِبّ أزورك ف المَغربيّة
أركَب فلوكة أنا وحَبايبي ونغَنّي غنْوة ع السُّمْسميّة
آه يا لالالي حَبيبي يا لالالي يا روحي يا لالالي
ع المَحلّة مُنين يا سَمنُودي ع المَحلّة مُنين ع أرْض جُدودي
ع المَحلّة مُنين آه يا شن ورن ع المَحلّة مُنين يا سَمنُودي
إسْكنْدريّة أحْسَن ناس ع البَحر ماشْية تتْمَخْتَر
من سيدي بشر لأبو العَبّاس أيوه يا عالم ع المَنْظَر
أيوه يا عالم ع المينا والشَوق بيتْمَرجَح بينا
وتلْتُميّة ألْف سَفينة ع البَحر ماشْية بتزَمَّر
يا نَقْرَزان حَيّ الجدْعان حَيّ العَرايس والعُرْسان
مَحروسة م الإنْس وم الجان يا حلْوة يا أمّ التَوب الأخْضَر
أمّا أنا، أنا من شُبْرا في مَصْر وأوْلادْها الطعْمين
زَيّ القَمَر بعْيون سَمْرا لابْسين عُقود فُلّ وياسْمين
والنِيل بيضْحَك ويغَنّي فاكرْني وبْيسْأَل عَنّي
أروح له ألْقاه مسْتَنّي وجَنب منّه أحْسَن ناس
أحْسَن ناس

المفردات

the best	أَحْسَن
it's good for us to do	آدينا
to chat	دَرْدِش، يِدَرْدِش
what else do we have?	وَرانا إيه؟
to chat, recount	حَكى، يِحْكي
to get to know, to get acquainted with	اتْعَرَّف، يِتْعَرَّف
to be honored	اتْشَرَّف، يِتْشَرَّف
our fellow citizen	بَلَدينا
mawwal, a genre of sung poetry	مَوّال ج. مَواويل
tower	بُرْج ج. أَبْراج
young pigeon, squab	زَغْلول ج. زَغاليل
pigeon coop	برج الزغاليل
my father! (my uncle!) (oh!)	يا بوي
world (here: people)	عالم

hardworking	شَغَال/ة
to be cheap	رخِص، يِرْخَص
man	راجِل ج. رِجَالة
serious	جَد
responsible	حِمْل جبال
bridge	كوبري ج. كَباري
handkerchief	مَنْديل ج. مَناديل
to cause to blink	طَرَف، يُطْرُف
love	هَوى
sunset time	مَغْرِبِيَة
felucca	فلوكة
grandfather	جد ج. جُدود
to strut, swagger	اتْمَخْتَر، يِتْمَخْتَر
view	مَنْظَر ج. مَناظِر
port	مينا
to swing, sway	اتْمَرْجَح، يِتْمَرْجَح
to sail	مِشي، يِمشي (سفينة)
to play a wind instrument	زَمَّر، يِزَمَّر
quarter, district	حَي ج. أَحْياء
reliable and brave	جَدَع/ة ج. جِدْعان
bride	عَروسة ج. عَرايِس
groom	عَريس ج. عِرْسان
protected	مَحْروس/ة
human	إنْس
jinnis	جان
garment, dress	توب
sweet, delicious	طعِم/طِعْمة
dark-skinned	أَسْمَر/سَمْرا ج. سُمْر
necklace	عُقْد ج. عِقْدان
Arabian jasmine	فُل
jasmine	ياسْمين
to go	راح، يُروح

to find	لَقى، يِلْقى
to wait for	اِسْتَنَى، يِسْتَنَى
next to	جَنْب

ملاحظات

١- آدينا بندردش، ورانا إيه؟

Let's just chat, what else do we have to do?

The expression (آدينـا + present-tense verb) is used to persuade someone to keep doing a particular action, implying that it is good or useful. For example:

عايز تمشي ليه؟ آدينا بنشوف أفلام وبنتسلى

Why do you want to leave? At least we're watching movies and having fun together!

(آدينـا) also could mean "here we are" in other contexts, as in this example: ارتاحـي خـلاص آدينـا ماشـيين meaning "I hope you'll calm down now that we're leaving." You can also change the personal pronoun after "آدي" to address different persons.

٢- أحسن ناس

The best people

This is a common reply Egyptians give when asked which country or town they're from, whether they know you or the place well or not.

٣- سوهاج يا بوي

Sohag, my friend

(بوي) is an Upper Egyptian word that is equivalent to (بابا), Father. It can be said respectfully to any man, even if they're not the speaker's father.

٤- نغني غنوة ع السمسمية

Sing a song with the simsimiya

The *simsimiya* is a traditional lyre-shaped musical instrument played in the cities and towns near Sinai, such as Port Said, Ismailia, and Suez.

٥- ع المحلة منين آه يا شن ورن

How do we get to Mahalla, O famous city

(شـن ورن) and (شـنة ورنـة) are used interchangeably to express someone's fame and good reputation. The word (شـنة) is derived from an ancient Egyptian word that means "an inquiry" while (رنـة) is an Arabic word that means "a ring" or "ringing" (sound). Thus, a controversial subject is said to cause a *shanna w-ranna*, but more commonly in modern usage, *shanna w-ranna* refers to fame in a positive manner. For example:

الدكتور ده له شنة ورنة في إسكندرية

This doctor is well-known in Alexandria.

٦- أيوه يا عالم ع المنظر

Oh, everyone, what a sight

(أيـوه) is an Alexandrian word equivalent to (يـاه) in the Cairene dialect. Both are exclamations of amazement.

٧- أما أنا، أنا من شبـرا في مصر

As for me, I am from Shubra in Egypt
Dalida was from Shubra, a district in Cairo.

التدريبات

١. حط علامة صح أو غلط قدام الجمل دي.

أ- الشاعر عايز يتعرف على كل المصريين. ( )

ب- سوهاج جنب الإسكندرية على البحر المتوسط. ( )

ت- الشاعر قابل حبيبته على كوبري بنها. ( )

ث- أحسن وقت تركب فيه الفلوكة هو الفجرية. ( )

ج- جدود الشاعر من المحلة. ( )

٢. كمل الجمل دي بكلمات من عندك.

أ- أنا شفت المدرس ده كتير بس لسه ما .... ش عليه.

ب- .... آلة موسيقية مشهورة في الإسماعيلية.

ت- سمنود في .... وسيدي بشر وأبو العباس في إسكندرية.

ث- ممكن نستورد حاجات من أوروبا عشان فيه .... في إسكندرية.

ج- رحنا الملاهي النهارده وقعدنا .... لحد المغربية.

٣. اختار الكلمة الصحيحة من بين الأقواس.

أ– بص الفرس الجميل ده ماشي .... (يتمرجح – يتمختر – يتعرف)

ب– .... يعني أغنية طويلة تقليدية. (غنوة – موال – سمسمية)

ت– بعض الهدوم .... في فترة الخصومات. (بتغلى – بترخص – بتفرفش)

ث– إيه رأيك تيجي البيت عندنا شوية و................ قبل ما ننام؟ (ندردش – نزور – نركب فلوكة)

ج– العربيات .... كتير قوي في القاهرة. (بتتمرجح – بتتمختر – بتزمر)

٤. استخرج من النص:
فعلين ماضيين

....
....

١٠ أفعال مضارعة

....
....
....
....
....
....
....
....
....
....

٤ أسماء فاعل

....
....
....
....

ووضّح الفرق بين الأفعال المضارعة وأسماء الفاعل.

....
....

٥. حط كل الأفعال المضارعة في جمل من عندك.

....

٦. اوصف الصورة دي.

يا بتاع النعناع

٢٠١٥

كلمات وألحان: عزيز الشافعي - غناء: مصطفى حجاج

This is a popular song that Egyptians play at wedding parties, as it uses expressions of flirtation using simple words.

يا بْتاع النُّعْناع يا مُنَعْنَع يا مُنَعْنَع
هات هديَة للمِتْدَلِّع اتْدَلَّع اتْدَلَّع
اللي سايِب قَلْبي يِوَلَّع وبْعَذاب قَلْبي بيِتْمَتَّع
وأما آجي أقول له أقابْلَك يِتْمَنَّع يِتْمَنَّع
يا بْتاع النُّعْناع يا مُنَعْنَع إنْتَ يا مُنَعْنَع
نور عيني قَلْبي من جُوَه مين غيرُه وغيرُه مين هُوَّ
ده تاعِبْني وبِرْضُه عاجِبْني وَلا حَوْل لِيَا وَلا قوة
يا بْتاع السُّكَّر يا مُسَكَّر يا مُسَكَّر يا مُسَكَّر
ليل نَهار في حبيبي بافَكَّر يا مُسَكَّر يا مُسَكَّر
طال غيابه عَلَيَا وكتَّر أكْتَر من كده مش هاقْدِر
وأما آجي أقول له أقابْلَك بيِكْبَر بيِكْبَر
يا بْتاع السِّمْسِم يا مُسَمْسِم يا مُسَمْسِم يا مُسَمْسِم
القوام حلو ومِتْقَسَّم مِتْقَسَّم مِتْقَسَّم
لَمَّا عِطْرُه الحلو يِنْسِم الحياة في وِشِّي بِتْبْتِسِّم
وَأَمَّا آجي أقول لُه أقابْلَك بيِأَفْلِم بيِأَفْلِم
يا بْتاع النُّعْناع يا مُنَعْنَع إنْتَ يا مُنَعْنَع
هات هديَة للمِتْدَلِّع اتْدَلَّع اتْدَلَّع
يا بْتاع السُّكَّر يا مُسَكَّر يا مُسَكَّر يا مُسَكَّر
ليل نَهار في حبيبي بافَكَّر يا مُسَكَّر يا مُسَكَّر

المفردات

mint seller	بتاع النعناع
minty	منعنع
give	هات
gift, present	هدية ج. هدايا
flirty, spoiled	متدلع
to flirt, pamper	اتدلع
to leave	ساب، يسيب
heart	قلب ج. قلوب
to light, fire, burn	ولَع، يولع
torture	عذاب
to enjoy	اتمتع، يتمتع
when	لما
to be about to do something	ييجي + فعل مضارع
to meet	قابل، يقابل
to refuse, decline	امتنع، يتمنع
someone else	غيره
also	برضه
to please	عجب، يعجب
I'm completely powerless, I can do nothing	لا حول ليا ولا قوة
sugar seller	بتاع السكر
sweet	مسكر
day and night	ليل نهار
to think	فكر، يفكر
absence	غياب
to increase	كَتَّر، يِكَتَّر
to ignore	كَبَّر، يِكَبَّر
sesame seller	بتاع السِمسِم
pretty, handsome	مِسَمسِم
body (of person)	قوام

proportionate	متقسم
perfume, scent	عطر ج. عطور
blow (like a breeze), diffuse	نَسَّم، يِنَسَّم
smile	اتْبَسَّم، يِتْبَسَّم

ملاحظات

١- يا بتاع النعناع

(بتاع) is typically used like "of" in English, as in the sentence:
The book of the student, or the book is the student's.

الكتاب بتاع الطالب.

It has feminine and plural forms which are (بتاعة) and (بتوع). Here, (بتاع) means the one who sells; it appears in the titles of some professions and vocations, such as:
The teacher who teaches Arabic.

المدرس بتاع العربي.

The engineer who repairs computers.

المهندس بتاع الكمبيوتر.

٢- للي سايب قلبي يولع

(اللي) is a relative pronoun that can be used to refer to masculine, feminine, and plural nouns.
This is the book which I bought yesterday.

ده الكتاب اللي اشتريته إمبارح.

This is the cat I like.

ده القطة اللي بحبها.

These are the people I met.

دول الناس اللي قابلتهم.

٣- بيأفلم بيأفلم

To tell lies, to act and pretend
Arabic, like many other languages, adopts some foreign words and 'Arabizes' them by adapting them to its own linguistic and grammatical forms. Here, (أفلم), which is derived from the English word "film," could be treated

like any other form IV verb (أفعل), including conjugating it. Other foreign words Arabized by Egyptians include (كَنْسِل، يكنسِل) which means and comes from the word "cancel."

التدريبات

١. حط علامة صح أو غلط قدام الجمل دي.

أ- حبيبة الشاعر بتتمتع بعذاب قلبه. ( )

ب- حبيبة الشاعر مهتمة جدا إنها تقابله. ( )

ت- بتاع النعناع بييع سكر. ( )

ث- الشاعر مابيفكرش في حبيبته خالص. ( )

ج- الشاعر عايز يجيب هدية لحبيبته. ( )

٢. كمل الجمل دي بكلمات من عندك.

أ- الراجل .... الفاكهة مش موجود النهارده، ممكن نشتري بسبوسة.

ب- عايز أشرب شاي بـ................. عشان منعش.

ت- الفيلم ده مش .... مابحبوش خالص.

ث- الكيك ده .... قوي والسكر الكتير مش كويس عشاني.

ج- أنا .... كتير قبل ما أنام وساعات مابعرفش أنام من التفكير.

٣. اختار الكلمة الصحيحة من بين الأقواس.

أ- إنت مش................. تشيل الدولاب ده لوحدك طبعًا. (هات - هتقدر - عاجبني)

ب- البسكويت ده ناشف من بره وطري من .... (جوه - بره - غيره)

ت- .... لنا لو سمحت بعشرة جنيه نعناع. (آجي - يتمتع - هات)

ث- حطينا الكنافة في الفرن ونسينا .... قبل ما نحطها. (نمتعه - نولعه - ندلعه)

ج- وافقت على خطوبتنا لكن كل ما بقولها نخرج .... (بتتمتع - بتتمنع - بتولع)

٤. استخرج من النص:

فعلين أمر

....

فعل في المستقبل

....

٣ اسم فاعل

....

....

٩ أفعال مضارعة

....

....

....

....

....

....

....

....

صفة أفعل التفضيل

....

٥.   حط الكلمات دي في جمل من عندك:

عطر - اتدلَع - اتمتَع - ولَع - أفلم - كبر - تاعبني

....

....

....

....

....

....

٦. اوصف الصورة دي.

....
....
....
....

١٩

عايزين بابا

١٩٨٤

كلمات: بخيت بيومي - ألحان: عمّار الشريعي - غناء: كورس الأطفال

This song first appeared in the TV series "غدًا تتفتّح الزهـور" (Tomorrow the Flowers Will Bloom), which tells the story of three children whose father abandoned them and moved abroad. The children grow to love their private tutor and, in this touching song, imagine what life would be like if he were their father.

ليه إنْتَ ماطْلِعْتِش بابا وتْخَلّيك عَلى طول وَيَانا
كُنَا نُشوفَك طول اليوم فـ الصُبْحِيَّة وقَبْل النَّوم
ما تْخَلّيك عَلى طول وَيَانا؟ عايْزين بابا يِبْقى مَعانا
عايْزين بابا يِبْقى مَعانا يا ريتَك بابا والأُسْتاذ

مالْناش بابا وعايْزين بابا وإنْتَ بابا بالنِّسبالنا
بتْعَلِّمْنا طَعْم الحُبّ وأَحْلى هديَّة بتْجيبْها لنا
حَتّى الكلْمة الصَّعْبة عَلينا بكُلّ سُهولة بتِشْرَحْها لنا
ما تْخَلّيك عَلى طول وَيَانا؟ عايْزين بابا يِبْقى مَعانا
عايْزين بابا يِبْقى مَعانا ياريتَك بابا والأُسْتاذ

إنْتَ كأنَّك بابا وأَكْتَر إنْتَ حنيّن إنْتَ بَرْضُه عَلينا
إنْتَ الغِنْوة اللي نغَنّيها وإنْتَ الحُبّ اللي مدَفّينا
حَبّيْتنا فـ الدُّنيا وشُفْنا كُلّ الدُّنيا زُهور حَوالينا
ما تْخَلّيك عَلى طول وَيَانا؟ عايْزين بابا يِبْقى مَعانا
عايْزين بابا يِبْقى مَعانا ياريتَك بابا والأُسْتاذ

شُفْنا الدُّنْيا جَميلة جَميلة واتْعَلِّمْنا الحُب مَعاك
كُنّا نُشوفَك قَبْل ما تيجي وإنْتَ تُشوفْنا وإنْتَ هناك
حَتّى إن رُحْت بعدْت وغِبْت ساعة الدَّرْس هَنِسْتَنّاك
ما تْخَلّيك عَلى طول وَيَانا؟ عايْزين بابا يِبْقى مَعانا
عايْزين بابا يِبْقى مَعانا ياريتَك بابا والأُسْتاذ

المفردات

to be, become	طِلِع، يِطْلَع
always	عَلى طول
with us	وَيَانا
to see	شاف، يُشوف
the whole day	طول اليوم
morning	الصُّبْحية = الصُّبْح
before (opposite: after)	قَبْل (العكس: بَعْد)
sleep	نوم
to want	عايِز ج. عايْزين
I/we wish	ياريت
teacher	أُسْتاذ ج. أَساتْذة
to teach	عَلِّم، يِعَلِّم
taste	طَعْم
to bring	جاب، يِجيب
even	حَتّى
word	كِلْمة ج. كِلْمات
hard, difficult	صَعْب/ة ج. صُعاب
ease	سُهولة
to explain	شَرَح، يِشْرَح
as if	كأن
affectionate	حَنَيِّن ج. حَنَيِّنين
also	بَرْضُه
warming	مدَفِّي
to make someone love something or someone else	حَبِّب، يِحَبِّب

flower	زَهْرة ج. زُهور
around us	حَوالينا
to learn	اتْعَلِّم، يِتْعَلِّم
to go	راح، يُروح
to go far away, to move away	بِعد، يِبْعِد
to miss, to be absent	غاب، يغيب
at the time of	ساعة
lesson	دَرْس ج. دُروس
to wait for	اسْتَنَّى، يِسْتَنَّى

ملاحظات

١- ما تخلّيك على طول ويّانا

Why don't you stay with us forever?

The construction (ما + فعل مضارع من غير بـ) has the meaning of "Why don't you/we . . . .?" and so can be used to make suggestions. Other examples include:

Why don't you drink your tea?

ما تشرب الشاي بتاعك؟

Why don't you come with me to the cinema?

ما تيجي معايا السينما؟

Why doesn't he go to sleep early?

ما يدخل ينام بدري؟

٢- عايزين بابا يبقى معانا

We want Dad to be with us

(يبقى) can be used interchangeably with (يكون) for the present tense of the verb "to be."

٣- مالْناش بابا وعايزين بابا وإنت بابا بالنَّسبالنا

We have no father, we want a father, and you are a father to us

Here, (بالنَّسبالنا) means "to us," as in "as far as we are concerned," or "in our opinion." When you add a suffix to the noun (نِسبة), the (ة) changes into an alif. This word can take the preposition (ـلِ) and personal pronouns, and in such a case the last letter would be changed as shown in the following table:

First person (sing.)	بالنِّسْبالي
Second person (masc.)	بالنِّسْبالَك
Second person (fem.)	بالنِّسْبالك
Third person (masc., sing.)	بالنِّسْبالُه
Third person (fem., sing.)	بالنِّسْبالُها
First person (pl.)	بالنِّسْبالْنا
Second person (pl.)	بالنِّسْبالْكو
Third person (pl.)	بالنِّسْبالْهم
Sometimes people just right the two words separated as "بالنسبة لي"	

٤- حتى إن رحت بعدت وغبت ساعة الدرس هنستناك

Even if you went far away and missed our lesson, we would wait for you
In the song, this sentence conveys a conditional meaning: "Even if you . . . we would . . ."
It uses the verb after (إن) in the past tense (رحت، بعدت، غبت) and the next verb is in the future tense (هنستناك), in accordance with the rule for conditional sentences.
It also uses a metaphor: referring to the tutor as the sun by use of the verb (غبت).

التّدريبات

١.   حطّ علامة صحّ أو غلط قدّام الجمل دي.

أ- لو الأستاذ كان أبوهم كانوا هيشوفوه الصبح وبالليل.   ( )

ب- الأستاذ بيشرح لهم أي كلمة صعبة بسهولة.   ( )

ت- أبو الأولاد دول مات.   ( )

ث- الأولاد اتعلموا الحب من أستاذهم.   ( )

ج- مهما بعد الأستاذ، الأولاد ساعة الدرس هيستنوه.   ( )

٢.   كمّل الجمل دي بكلمات من عندك.

أ- عمري ما دقت .... الحب إلا لما قابلتك.

ب- أختي مش أختي وبس، دي .... لي صاحبتي كمان.

ت- إيه أجمل .... جات لك في عيد ميلادك؟

ث- المدرس ده بيشرح كل قواعد العربي ....

ج- باحب قوي أوضتك عشان ريحة .... اللي مالياها.

٣.   اختار الكلمة الصحيحة من بين الأقواس.

أ- سمعت شوية موسيقى .... خلوا يومي جميل.   (الصبحية - قبل النوم - الحب)

ب- .... يا ماما قاعدة شوية معانا، هتمشي بدري ليه؟   (ما تغني - ما تخليكي - حوالينا)

ت- سكرتير الشركة بيعاملني .... مديري.   (لإنه - كإنه - يبقى)

ث- هنصور الفيلم إزاي بعد ما الشمس ....   (شافت - ياريت - غابت)

ج- .... بابا كان فضل معانا.   (حنيّن - مدّفينا - ياريت)

٤.   حطّ الكلمات دي في جمل من عندك:

طعم - الصَّبحيَة - ياريت - ما تخلَيك - بالنَسبة - استنّى

....

....

....

....

....

٥.   استخرج من النص:

اسم فاعل

....

الكلمات المنفية

....

كلمة في حالة الجمع

....

صفة على وزن أفعل

....

كل الصفات

....

....

....

....

....
....
....
....
....

٢٠

إزاي

٢٠١٠

كلمات: نصر الدين ناجي - ألحان: أحمد فرحات - غناء: محمد منير

Although Mohamed Mounir recorded this song in late 2010, it gained popularity during the 2011 revolution. Its lyrics seemed at that time realistic and relatable, touching the hearts of many Egyptians.

إزَاي تِرْضي لي حَبيبْتي أَتْمَعْشَق اسْمك وإنْتي
عَمَّالة تزيدي في حيرْتي ومانْتيش حاسَّة بطيبْتي إزَاي؟
مش لاقي في عشْقك دافِع وَلا صدْقي في حُبَّك شافِع
إزَاي أَنا رافِع راسك وإنْتي بتحْني في راسي إزَاي؟
أَنا أَقْدم شارِع فيكي وآمالك م اللي باليكي
أَنا طِفْل اتْعَلَّق بيكي في نُصّ السِّكَّة وتَوَّهْتيه
أَنا لو عاشْقك متْخَيَّر كان قَلْبي زَمانه اتْغَيَّر
وحياتك لأَفْضل أغَيَّر فيكي لحد ما تِرْضي عَليه
إزَاي تِرْضي لي حَبيبْتي أَتْمَعْشَق اسْمك وإنْتي
عَمَّالة تزيدي في حيرْتي ومانْتيش حاسَّة بطيبْتي إزَاي؟
مش لاقي في عشْقك دافِع وَلا صدْقي في حُبَّك شافِع
إزَاي أَنا رافِع راسك وإنْتي بتحْني في راسي إزَاي؟
إزَاي سايْباني في ضَعْفي؟ طب ليه مش واقْفة في صَفِّي
وَأَنا عِشْت حَياتي بحالْها عَشان مالْمَحْش في عينك خوف؟
وفْ بَحْرك وَلا ف بَرَّك إزَاي أَحْمي لك ضَهْرك
وَأَنا ضَهْري في آخِر الليل دايْماً بيبَات مَحْني ومَكْشوف؟
أَنا أَقْدم شارِع فيكي وآمالك م اللي باليكي
أَنا طِفْل اتْعَلَّق بيكي في نُصّ السِّكَّة وتَوَّهْتيه

أَنا لو عاشْقِك مِتْخَيَّر كان قَلْبي زَمانُه اتْغَيَّر
وحياتِك لَأُفْضَل أَغَيَّر فيكي لِحَد ما تِرْضي عَليه
إِزَّاي تِرْضي لي حَبيبْتي أَتْمَعْشَق اسْمِك وإنْتي
عَمَّالة تزيدي في حيرْتي وماِنْتيش حاسَة بِطيبْتي إِزَّاي؟
مِش لاقي في عِشْقِك دافِع وَلا صِدْقي في حُبِّك شافِع
إِزَّاي أَنا رافِع راسِك وإنْتي بِتِحْني في راسي إِزَّاي؟

المفردات

to accept, to be satisfied or content	رضي، يرضى	
to love	اتمعشق، يتمعشق	
to keep doing	عمال	
to increase	زاد، يزيد	
confusion	حيرة	
to feel	حس، يحس	
goodness, kindheartedness	طيبة	
to find	لقى، يلقى	
love, passion	عشق	
motivation	دافع ج. دوافع	
sincerity, truthfulness	صدق	
to mediate, intercede	شفع، يشفع	
to raise, lift	رفع، يرفع	
head	راس	
to bend, turn	حنى، يحني	
hope	أمل ج. آمال	
to make someone suffer, to make something old	بلى، يبلي	
to get attached to, to be fond of	اتعلق، يتعلق بـ	
half	نص ج. إنصاص	
way	سكة ج. سكك	
to mislead, lead astray	توّه، يتوّه	
to passionately love	عشق، يعشق	
being able to choose	متخير/ة	

to change (reflexive)	اتغير، يتغير
to keep doing	فضل، يفضل
to change	غير، يغير
to leave, let	ساب، يسيب
weakness, feebleness	ضعف
on someone's side, supporting	في صف
the whole of it	بحالها
to glance	لمح، يلمح
fear	خوف
land	بر
to protect	حمى، يحمي
to spend the night	بات، يبات

ملاحظات

١- مانتيش حاسة بطيبتي؟

Don't you feel my kindheartedness?

This is an example of how a sentence can be a negated one by negating a pronoun.

(I am not)	مانيش
(You (fem.) are not)	مانتيش
(You (masc.) are not)	مانتاش
(You (pl.) are not)	مانتوش
(We are not)	ماحناش

٢- عمالة تزيدي في حيرتي

You keep increasing my confusion

(عمّال) is an adjective that can be followed by a verb in the present tense to mean "to keep doing" something. The verb will often start with (بـ). It is usually used to express disapproval or frustration.

Why do you keep watching movies and leaving your homework?

عمال بتتفرج على أفلام وسايب مذاكرتك ليه؟

I keep calling him but he does not pick up.

أنا عمال أتصل بيه مابيردش.

٣- أنا لو عاشقك متخير

If I love you, it's by choice

(متخيـر) is a formal modern standard Arabic word that is rarely heard in Egyptian colloquial Arabic. But modern standard Arabic words are sometimes used in colloquial poetry for reasons of style and rhyme.

٤- وحياتك لأفضل أغير فيكي

By your life, I will keep changing you

(لـ) + (وحياتك) + (و) + a present tense verb allows someone to swear on something. (وحياتك) literally means "and by your life," and here the poet swears on Egypt's life. (والله) means to swear by God, and (والنبـي) to swear on the Prophet.

I swear to God, I will stop smoking cigarettes.

والله لأبطل السجاير.

٥- وأنا عشت حياتي بحالها

I have lived my whole life

In spoken Egyptian, (وأنا) can be pronounced without the *hamza* (أ), as if it were spelled (وَنا).

التدريبات

١. حط علامة صح أو غلط قدام الجمل دي.
أ- الشاعر سعيد قوي في بلده.   (   )
ب- الأغنية دي اتغنت بعد ثورة ٢٥ يناير ٢٠١١.   (   )
ت- الأغنية دي وطنية.   (   )
ث- الشاعر زعلان جدًا من بلده.   (   )
ج- الشاعر مابقاش يحب بلده.   (   )

٢. كمل الجمل دي بكلمات من عندك.
أ- إنت مكسوف ليه؟ .... راسك وإنت ماشي.
ب- .... بين الهرم والقلعة تاخد وقت قد إيه؟

ت- الجيش هو اللي .... البلد.

ث- إنتو هتسافروا بالليل بـ .... ولا البحر؟

ج- .... هو أهم حاجة في الصداقة، لو مش موجود تبقى دي مش صداقة.

٣. اختار الكلمة الصحيحة من بين الأقواس.

أ- هي اتجوزت الراجل ده بالذات عشان .... حيرته)	(طيبته – خوفه –
ب- صاحبي هو الوحيد اللي وقف معايا في لحظات .... عشقي)	(صدقي – ضعفي –
ت- المسرحية .... ساعة ونص بس، مش طويلة قوي يعني. بحالها)	(شافع – اتمعشق –
ث- ممكن .... عندك النهارده عشان النور قاطع عندي؟ أتوَه)	(أبات – أعشق –
ج- نفسي أذاكر في الأجازة بس للأسف ماعنديش أي .... خوف)	(عشق – دافع –

٤. حط الكلمات دي في جمل من عندك:

عمَّال - فِضل - اتغير - غير - ساب - في صف - رفع رضي

....

....

....

....

....

....

٥. استخرج من النص:

صفة على وزن أفعل التفضيل

....

٧ أسماء فاعل

....

اسمي مفعول

....

٤ أفعال مضارعة من غير (ب)

....

فعلين مضارعين مع (ب)

....

كل الأفعال الماضية

....

جملة شرط

....

٦. اوصف الصورة دي.

....

Grammar Reference

Lesson one

The Present Tense (زمن المضارع/الحالي): Indicative and Subjunctive

In Egyptian colloquial Arabic, the present tense has two different forms: the indicative and the subjunctive. The indicative takes the prefix (بِ) and is the most commonly used form of present tense verbs. It expresses actions that actually happen in reality. For example:

- An action happening right now (I am running – أنا باجري).
- An action or state that regularly happens (I sit in this chair everyday - أنا باقعد ع الكرسي ده كل يوم).
- Something that is generally true (falcons fly – الصقور بتطير).

The subjunctive does not take the prefix (بِ) and is used to describe things that do not necessarily happen in reality. It is often used to describe actions or states that may, could, or should happen, or to describe the idea of an action rather than a specific instance of it.

This can be hard to conceptualize so let's have a look at a few examples. Take the sentence "I read a book every Friday" which could be translated as "أنا باقرا كتاب كل يوم جمعة." The verb is indicative because the "reading" happens in reality every Friday. Similarly, "I am reading," or "أنا باقرا" is indicative because it is happening in reality, right now.

"I like coffee," or "أنا باحب القهوة," is also indicative although it is not a recurring action in the same way that reading on Friday is because the "liking" is still happening in real life right now, even though in a few years you might stop liking coffee, but in all cases, the fact is you like coffee at this moment.

How about "I like drawing comics," or "أنا باحِب أرسِم الكوميكس؟" As with the coffee example, "like" here is indicative and happens in reality. But how about "drawing?" You are not telling us that you regularly draw or that you are drawing now. We also do not know if you ever drew comics. You are not talking about a real-life instance of drawing; you are merely talking about the idea of drawing. This is what makes "drawing" in this case subjunctive.

Let's look at another example. "I am opening the window," or "أنـا بافْتَح الشِّبّاك." This is indicative because the "opening" is taking place right now in reality. Let's compare it with "Should I open the window?" or "أَفْتَح الشِّبّاك؟": Does the "opening" actually happen or not? We do not know. I am not describing a real occurrence of a window being opened; I am just talking about the idea of opening it.

Indicative		
Actually happens in reality. Takes the prefix (بِـ)		
(i) Happens right now:	Mum is listening to music right now.	دلوقتي ماما بتسمع موسيقى.
	We're watching TV (now). How about you; what are you doing?	إحنا بنتفرج على التلفزيون، إنتو بتعملوا إيه؟
	Give me a second because I'm writing a message.	ثواني عشان باكتب رسالة.
	We're not eating right now; we're listening to songs.	إحنا مش بناكل دلوقتي، إحنا بنسمع أغاني.
(ii) Happens regularly:	I go to work every day at 8 a.m.	أنا باروح كل يوم الشُغل السّاعة ٨ الصّبح.
	At what time do you usually set your alarm?	إنت بتظبَط المنبّه على السّاعة كام في العادة؟
	Does the shop open every day?	هو المحل بيفتح كل يوم؟
	Why don't you do your homework on a daily basis?	إنتوا مابتعملوش الواجب ليه كل يوم؟
	Why don't you eat with me every day?	إنت مابتاكلش معايا ليه كل يوم؟

	They don't go to the cinema at night.	هم **مش بيروحوا** سينما بالليل.
	My sister doesn't like chocolate.	أختي **مابتحبِّش** الشوكولاتة.
	The student is studying four languages at the university.	الطَّالب **بيدرس** أربع لغات في الجامعة.
(iii) General statements and facts:	The earth revolves around the sun.	الأرض **بتلفّ** حوالين الشَّمس.
	Egyptians eat cookies during Eid al-Fitr, the feast following Ramadan.	المصريِّين **بياكلوا** كحك في العيد الصُّغيَّر.
	Brazilians speak Portuguese.	البرازيليَين **بيتكلَّموا** برتغالي.
	These Canadians don't speak English, they speak French.	الكنديين دول **مابيتكلموش** إنجليزي، **بيتكلموا** فرنساوي.
(iv) Reasons—when (عشان) conveys the meaning of "because"	I am studying Arabic because I love it.	أنا **بادرس** عربي عشان **باحب** العربي.

Subjunctive

Does not necessarily happen in reality but may, could, or should happen.
Does not take the prefix (بِ)

	Would you like to go to the cinema today?	**تحبَّ نروح** سينما النَّهارده؟
	Shall we travel to Europe in the summer?	**تيجي نسافر** أوروبا في الصيف؟
(i) Suggestions:	Would you like to watch a movie or listen to music together?	**نشوف** فيلم ولّا **نسمع** موسيقى؟
	Let's drink tea on the balcony!	يالّا **نشرب** الشَّاي في البلكونة!

(ii) Possibility and probability:	We might probably watch a movie together tonight.	احتمال **نتفرج** على فيلم مع بعض الليلة دي.
	I might go to Alexandria tomorrow; I'm still not sure.	ممكن **أروح** إسكندرية بكرة، مش متأكد.
(iii) Attempts:	I tried to carry the heavy bag.	حاولت **أشيل** الشَنطة التَقيلة.
(iv) Requests:	Can you remove these dishes?	ممكن **تشيل** الأطباق دي؟
	Can I open the window?	ممكن **أفتح** الشُباك؟
(v) Obligations and necessity:	We have to study a lot to be able to learn Arabic.	لازم **نذاكر** كتير عشان نتعلَم العربي.
(vi) Prayers:	Speaker A: Do you want anything else? Speaker B: No thanks. God bless you.	المتحدث أ: عايز حاجة تانية؟ المتحدث ب: شكرًا ربنا **يخليك**!
(vii) Wishes or desires:	I hope we can eat something new today.	يا ريت **ناكل** حاجة جديدة النَهارده.
	I wish I could go to France and study French.	نفسي **أروح** فرنسا **وأدرس** فرنساوي.
	I hope you have fun on the trip.	**أتمنى تستمتع** في الرحلة.
	I want to drink tea.	**عايز** أشرب شاي.
(viii) Reasons—when (عشان) conveys the meaning of "in order to":**	I came to Egypt to study Arabic.	أنا جيت مصر عشان **أتعلم** عربي.
	We went (into the bedroom) to sleep for a bit.	إحنا دخلنا (عشان) **ننام** شوية.

(ix) After another verb (except for كان):	Huda forgot to take the key with her.	هدى نسيت **تاخُد** المفتاح معاها.
	Can you swim?	إنت بتعرف **تعوم**؟
	We're thinking of going to the cinema.	إحنا بنفكَّر **نروح** سينما.
	I can carry this table by myself.	أنا أقدر **أشيل** التَّرابيزة دي لوحدي.
(x) After time expressions with (ما):	Did you eat before coming?	إنت كلت قبل ما **تيجي**؟
	As soon as you get home, email me.	أول ما **توصل** البيت ابعت لي الإيميل.
	After you finish your lesson, come see me.	بعد ما **تخلَّصي** الدَّرس عدّي عليا.

Verbs in the indicative and the subjunctive presents could be expressed in the negative by using them either with (مِش) or with the prefix (ما) and the suffix (ش). For example:

بادْرِس — مش بادْرِس / مابادْرِسْش
باحِبّ — مش باحِبّ / ماباحِبِّش
أدْرِس — مش أدْرِس / مادْرِسْش
أحِبّ — مش أحِبّ / ماحِبِّش

(عشــان), which is used to convey reasons, can either mean "because" or "in order to." If it means "because," the indicative is used in Arabic. When it means "in order to," the subjunctive is used in Arabic, as shown in the table.

The Future Tense (زمن المستقبل)

The future tense is formed by adding the prefix (هَـ) to the present tense. For example:

يِشْرَب — هَيِشْرَب

Note that in the first person singular (أنا), the hamza is dropped from the alif.

أَشْرَب — هاشْرَب

If the second letter of the stem (the part after letter (ي) in the present tense form) is a long vowel or a doubled consonant, then the short vowel before it will be deleted when the prefix (هَـ) is added.

(long vowel)   يِنام — هَيْنام

(long vowel)	يَقول — هَيْقول
(long vowel)	بِيبيع — هَيْبيع
(long vowel)	يِسافر — هَيْسافر
(doubled consonant)	يِشِدّ — هَيْشِدّ

The Imperative (فعل الأمر)

The imperative (فعل الأمر) is used to give orders or instructions. For example, "Close the window!" (اقفل الشباك) and "Shut the door!" (اقفل الباب) are both in the imperative.

In Arabic, we form the imperative by taking the present form of the verb and replacing the prefix with either (ا) or (أ) depending on the vowel pattern of the verb: If the second vowel in the stem is damma, then the alif we add will take a damma in the imperative (أ). If the second vowel in the stem is a fatha or a kasra, then the alif we add will take a kasra in the imperative (ا). For example:

Verb Meaning	Present Tense	Imperative
to open	يِفتَح	افْتَح
to explain	يِشرَح	اشْرَح
to go up, ascend	يِطلَع	اطْلَع
to put on, wear	يِلبِس	الْبِس
to write	يِكتِب	اكْتِب
to count	يِحسِب	احْسِب
to dance	يُرقُص	أُرقُص
to enter	يُدخُل	أُدخُل
to go out	يُخرُج	أُخرُج
to produce	يِنتِج	انْتِج
to direct	يِخرِج	اخْرِج
to get married	يِتجَوِّز	اتْجَوِّز
to enjoy	يِتمَتَّع	اتْمَتَّع
to meet	يِتقابِل	اتْقابِل
to overcome	يِنتِصِر	انْتِصِر
to spread	يِنتِشِر	انْتِشِر

to be affected, react	يِنْفِعِل	اِنْفِعِل
to enjoy	يِنْبِسِط	اِنْبِسِط
to use	يِسْتَخْدِم	اِسْتَخْدِم
to extract	يِسْتَخْرِج	اِسْتَخْرِج

Feminine and Plural Forms in the Imperative

Like in the present tense, the feminine form in the imperative is created by adding a (ي) to the end of the verb while the plural form in the imperative is created by adding (و) to the end of the verb.

Verb Meaning	Present Tense	Imperative
to drink	يِشْرَب	اِشْرَب، اِشْرَبِي، اِشْرَبوا
to order	يُطْلُب	أُطْلُب، أُطْلُبِي، أُطْلُبوا
to know	يِعْرَف	اِعْرَف، اِعْرَفِي، اِعْرَفوا
to hit	يِضْرَب	اِضرَب، اِضْرَبِي، اضربوا

Creating the Imperative from Present Tense Verbs with No *Sukun*

If the second letter of the present tense verb has no *sukun*—for example, as with verbs whose middle root letter is a vowel (like نام) or verbs with geminate second and third root letters (the last letter has a *shadda*) (like حَبّ)—then the imperative is created by deleting the prefix (يِ) from the present tense verb without adding the imperative alif prefix (ا) or (أ) as was previously mentioned. In verbs (ياكل) and (ياخد) we delete (يـ) and the letter after it (ا) not to start with a vowel, since Arabic words never start with a vowel.

Verb Meaning	Present Tense	Imperative
to sleep	يِنام	نام
to go	يُروح	روح
to sell	يِبيع	بيع
to pull	يِشدّ	شدّ
to love	يحبّ	حبّ
to shake (liquids)	يُرُجّ	رُجّ

to eat	ياكُل	كُل
to take	ياخُد	خُد
to prepare	يحَضَّر	حَضَّر
to teach	يعَلِّم	عَلِّم
to travel	يسافر	سافر
to meet	يقابل	قابل
to try	يحاول	حاول
to study	يذاكر	ذاكر

Example sentences:

Drink the tea, Ahmed!

اِشْرَب الشَّاي يا أَحْمَد!

Ring the bell, Nada!

اِضْرَبي الجَرَس يا نَدا!

Put the books in your bags, guys!

دَخَّلوا الكُتُب في الشُّنَط يا شَباب!

Move out of the way, kids!

وَسَّعوا السِّكة يا أولاد!

Play with the dog, Hassan!

اِلعَب مَع الكَلْب يا حَسَن!

Order me a pizza, Dad!

اُطْلُب لي بيتزا يا بابا!

The Negative Imperative (أسلوب النهي)

The negative imperative (أسلوب النهي) is identical in form to the negative present tense without (بـ), as shown in this table:

Negative Imperative	Imperative	Present	Verb
ماتِلْعَبْش	اِلعَب	تِلعَب	
ماتِلْعَبيش	اِلعَبي	تِلعَبي	لِعِب
ماتِلْعَبوش	اِلعَبوا	تِلعَبوا	

ماتْروحْش	روح	تُروح	
ماتْروحيش	روحي	تُروحي	راح
ماتْروحوش	روحوا	تُروحوا	
ماتْبُصِّش	بصَّ	تبصَّ	
ماتْبُصِّيش	بصِّي	تبصِّي	بَصَّ
ماتْبُصّوش	بصّوا	تبصّوا	

Example sentences:

ماتشربيش سجاير عشان إنت لسَّه صغيَّر.

Do not smoke cigarettes because you're still young.

ماتتأخروش برَّه يا ولاد.

Don't stay out late, kids!

ماتاكليش سمك كتير عشان مش كويس عشانك.

Don't eat too much fish because it isn't good for you!

ماتلعبش مع الكلب ده عشان ممكن يعضك.

Don't play with this dog because it might bite you.

ماتكتبوش في الكراسة دي، اكتبوا في الكراسة التَّانية.

Don't write in this notebook, write in the other one.

Active Participle 1 (اسم الفاعل)

Egyptian Arabic differentiates between states (الحـالات) and actions (الأفـعـال). Verbs are generally considered states when they do not involve movement or effort on the part of the subject, for example, sitting, hearing, seeing, or standing up. Verbs that involve movement or conscious effort are usually considered action verbs. For example, eating, writing, listening, or watching.

Actions happening at the time of speaking, like "I am running," are formed using the present tense indicative form of the verb, with (بِ). However, states happening at the time of speaking are formed with the active participle of the verb. The active participle is formed by putting the root of the verb into the pattern (فاعِل), as shown below:

فعل — فاعِل

to understand	فهِم — فاهِم
to ride	ركِب — راكِب
to write	كتَب — كاتِب
to open	فتَح — فاتِح

Some example sentences:
I *live* in Cairo.

أنا عايش/ساكن في القاهرة.

She *wants* tea.

هي عايزة شاي.

We *are sitting* on the sofa.

إحنا قاعدين عَ الكنبة.

They *are sleeping* now.

هم نايمين دلوقتي.

I *am awake* right now.

أنا صاحي دلوقتي.

He *is walking* down the street.

هو ماشي ف الشارع. (irregular)

Note that the verb (يمشـي) is an exception to the rule in that although it appears to describe an action, the active participle is used.

The feminine form of the active participle is formed by adding (ة) while the plural is formed by adding (ين):

ساكِن، ساكْنة، ساكْنين

living

عايِز، عايْزة، عايْزين

wanting

آسِف، أَسْفة، أَسْفين

being sorry

The active participle is negated using (مش). For example:
The girl isn't staying in the house.

البنت مش قاعْدة ف البيت.

The verbs most commonly used with the active participle are listed below:

المعنى (Meaning)	اسم الفاعل (Active Participle)	الفعل الماضي (Past Tense)
to stand	واقِف، واقْفة، واقْفين	وقف
to live (in a place)	ساكِن، ساكْنة، ساكْنين	سكن
to know	عارِف، عارْفة، عارْفين	عرف
to hear	سامِع، سامْعة، سامْعين	سمِع
to understand	فاهِم، فاهْمة، فاهْمين	فهِم
to ride	راكِب، راكْبة، راكْبين	ركِب

to wear	لابِس، لابْسة، لابْسين	لبِس
to sit down, stay	قاعِد، قاعْدة، قاعْدين	قَعَد
to lean against	سانِد، سانْدة، سانْدين	سَنَد
to drive	سايِق، سايْقة، سايْقين	ساق
to carry	شايِل، شايْلة، شايْلين	شال
to live	عايِش، عايْشة، عايْشين	عاش
to want	عايِز، عايْزة، عايْزين	عاز
to sleep	نايِم، نايْمة، نايْمين	نام
to see	شايِف، شايْفة، شايْفين	شاف
to smell	شامِم، شامَة، شامِّين	شَمَّ
to feel	حاسِس، حاسّة، حاسِّين	حَسَّ
to walk	ماشي، ماشْية، ماشْيين	مشِي
to forget	ناسي، ناسْية، ناسْيين	نسِي

Exercise 1: Translate these sentences into English.

١. إحْنا ماشْيين في الشّارع.

....

٢. كُلِّنا عايْزين ناكُل رُز.

....

٣. إنت فاهِم درس العربي؟

....

٤. أنا سامِع صوت عربيّات ف الشّارع.

....

٥. أختي واقْفة ف البلكونة.

....

٦. المُدَرِّسة لابْسة شيك قوي النّهارده.

....

٧. بابا نايِم من السّاعة عشرة.

....

٨. كلنا راكْبين المترو.

....

٩. أنا ساكِن ف المَعادي، وصاحْبتي ساكْنة ف الدُّقي.

....

١٠. بابا عايِش في ألمانيا، وماما عايْشة في أمريكا.

....

Exercise 2: Change these sentences from singular to plural or vice versa.

١. أنا مش سامِع صوت الرّاديو.

....

٢. البِنت مش قاعْدة ف البيت.

....

٣. إحنا مش شايْفين المدرّس، هو فين؟

....

٤. كلنا عايْزين شاي بلبن.

....

٥. إنتو مش عايْشين ف العاصمة؟

....

Active Participle 2 (اسم الفاعل)

The active participles of verbs containing more than 3 root letters are formed by removing the letter (بـ) from the present tense and replacing it with (مِـ). For example:

الفعل المضارع	اسم الفاعل
يسافِر	مسافِر، مسافْرة، مسافْرين
يهاجِر	مهاجِر، مهاجْرة، مهاجْرين
يسامِح	مسامِح، مسامْحة، مسامْحين
يقابِل	مقابِل، مقابْلة، مقابْلين
يخلّص	مخلّص، مخلّصة، مخلّصين
يعدّي	معدّي، معدّية، معدّيين
يزوّد	مزوّد، مزوّدة، مزوّدين
يعرّف	معرّف، معرّفة، معرّفين
يتْخرّج	متْخرّج، متْخرّجة، متْخرّجين
يتْجوّز	متْجوّز، متْجوّزة، متْجوّزين
يتْعرّف	متْعرّف، متْعرّفة، متْعرّفين
يسْتخْدِم	مسْتخْدِم، مسْتخْدِمة، مسْتخْدِمين
يسْتنّى	مسْتنّي، مسْتنّية، مسْتنّيين

Action Verbs and the Active Participle (اسم الفاعل)

In addition to the past tense (زمن الماضي), the active participle can also be used to describe actions that started in the past but whose effects continue into the present. For example, "أنا واكل سمك," or "I have eaten fish," indicates that you still feel the effect of the food that you ate (so you're not hungry or you don't want to eat fish again just yet, or you are still savoring the memory of the taste).

Other examples:

I've borrowed 20 pounds from him (e.g., and now he wants the money back, or I might borrow some more).

أنا واخد منه ٢٠ جنيه سلف.

Have you had something to drink? (e.g., you look drunk)

إنت شارب حاجة ولا إيه؟

I've bought food from the supermarket (e.g., the food is on the table).

أنا جايب أكل من السوبرماركت.

Movement Verbs

As well as being used to convey a continuous present (states) and a past meaning (actions), (اسـم الفاعـل) can also be used to convey the future tense for a small number of verbs which relate to moving locations. For example:

Are you getting off at the next stop?

إنتي نازلة المحطة الجاية؟

I'm traveling to Brazil on Sunday.

أنا مسافر البرازيل يوم الحد.

The movement verbs for which we can use the active participle are:

المعنى	اسم الفاعل	الفعل الماضي
to go	رايح، رايْحة، رايْحين	راح
to come	جاي، جايَة، جايْين	جه
to go down, get off	نازل، نازْلة، نازْلين	نزل
to go up, ascend	طالع، طالْعة، طالْعين	طلع
to go out, hang out	خارج، خارْجة، خارْجين	خرج
to enter	داخل، داخْلة، داخْلين	دخل
to travel	مسافر، مسافْرة، مسافْرين	سافر
to leave	ماشي، ماشْية، ماشْيين	مشي

It is important to note that these verbs, while appearing to be actions, are treated as states and are used with active participles (اسم الفاعل) rather than the indicative form of the present tense (بـ) when conveying a present continuous meaning.

I'm coming!

أنا جاي.

I'm going down the stairs.

أنا نازل ع السلم.

Note that verb (مشـي) has two meanings, first is to walk and second is to leave, if you say (ماشي) and you mean "to walk" it is translated in English as "he is walking," and if you say (ماشي) and you mean "to leave" it is translated in English as "he is going to leave or about to leave."

The active participle form of movement verbs can also be used to give a past meaning as described in the section above. This means that the active participle form of these verbs can indicate that an action happened either in the past, in the present, or in the future, and you must rely on the context to ascertain the tense.

I got back from Alexandria half an hour ago. (past)

أنا راجع من إسكندرية من نص ساعة.

I'm coming now! (present)

أنا جاي دلوقتي.

I'll come at 7 p.m. (future)

أنا جاي الساعة سبعة بالليل.

Passive Voice (المبني للمجهول)

Verbs with 3 root letters can be made passive by putting them into the pattern (اتْفَعَل) for the past and (يتْفِعل) for the present, as shown in this table:

المبني للمجهول		المبني للمعلوم	
(Passive)		(Active)	
يتْفِعل	اتْفَعَل	يفعل	فعل
يتْشرب	اتْشَرَب	يِشْرَب	شرب
يتْلعب	اتْلَعَب	يِلْعَب	لعب
يتْكتب	اتْكَتَب	يِكْتب	كَتَب
يتْفتح	اتْفَتَح	يِفْتَح	فَتَح
يتْفهم	اتْفَهَم	يِفْهَم	فهم
يتْعرف	اتْعَرَف	يِعْرَف	عرف
يتاكل (irregular)	اتاكل	ياكُل	كل

يتاخد (irregular)	اتاخد	ياخُد	خَد
يتْحَبّ	اتْحَبّ	يحبّ	حَبّ
يتْحَطّ	اتْحَطّ	يُحُطّ	حَطّ

Note that Egyptian Arabic tends not to use the passive voice if the subject is known. Sentences such as "Egypt was occupied by Britain for 74 years" would be usually translated as "بريطانيا احتلت مصر لـ٧٤ سنة" ("Britain occupied Egypt for 74 years").

Examples:

باين الباب اتفتح لوحده.

It appears the door was opened by itself.

الدرس خلاص اتشرح، مش هاشرح الدرس تاني.

The lesson has already been explained; I won't explain it again.

الإيميل ده اتكتب إمتى؟

When was this email written?

حكايتك مع نورا اتعرفت في كل مكان.

Everyone knows your story with Nora.

العربية بتاعتي اتصلَحت عند الميكانيكي ده.

My car was repaired in this mechanic shop.

الشنطة اتقطعت وأنا في الشارع، لازم أشتري واحدة جديدة.

The bag tore when I was on the street; I need to buy a new one.

"ألف ليلة وليلة" اتَرجمت لكل لغات العالم تقريبًا.

The Thousand and One Nights was translated into almost all languages.

الجامع ده اتبنى سنة كام؟

In what year was this mosque built?

الماتش هيتلعب بكرة إمتى وفين؟

When and where will the match be played tomorrow?

الأغنية دي اتغنت أكتر من مرة.

This song was sung more than once.

Passive Participle (اسم المفعول)

As with the active participle (اسم الفاعل), the passive participle (اسم المفعول) acts like a regular adjective.

مفعول		فعل	
drunk	مَشْروب	to drink	شرب
hit	مَضْروب	to hit	ضَرَب
known	مَعْروف	to know	عرف
written	مَكْتوب	to write	كَتَب
open	مَفْتوح	to open	فَتَح
printed	مَطْبوع	to print	طَبَع
accepted	مَقْبول	to accept	قبل
digested	مَهْضوم	to digest	هَضَم
loved	مَحْبوب	to love	حَبَّ

Examples:

الكتاب ده مكتوب إمتى؟

When was this book written?

الكاتب ده معروف في كل العالم.

This writer is famous all over the world.

هي الموسيقى الغربية محبوبة في مصر؟

Is Western music popular in Egypt?

كلامك مش مقبول.

What you're saying is not acceptable.

ليه نمت والشباك مفتوح؟

Why did you sleep with the window open?

الكيك معمول كويس قوي.

The cake was properly made.

الورد ده محطوط هنا ليه؟

Why have the roses been put here?

عايز أغير الجيتار ده عشان مكسور.

I want to change this guitar because it's broken.

اللوحة ده مرسومة في القرن التسعتاشر.

This painting was drawn in the nineteenth century.

الأكل النهارده مش مطبوخ كويس، هو الشيف جديد ولا إيه؟

The food isn't properly cooked today; is the chef new?

Ordinal Numbers

1 to 10

The number one has an irregular ordinal number: (أوّل), for the masculine, and (أولـى), for the feminine.

From 2 to 10, the ordinal numbers are formed by putting the root letters of the cardinal number into the (فاعِل) pattern. For example: تلاتة (three) — تالِت (third).

In addition, from 2 to 10, the noun associated with the ordinal number is in singular form. For example: قطتين (two cats) — تاني قطة (the second cat).

There are two ways of using the ordinal numbers from 1 to 10:
- When the ordinal number is before the noun, the ordinal number will always be in the masculine form and both the noun and the number will be indefinite.
- When the ordinal number is after the noun, the number is used as an adjective, following the noun in gender and grammatical definiteness (التعريف).

Cardinal Number	Ordinal Number Before the Noun	Ordinal Number After the Noun
بيت واحد (One house)	أول بيت (The first house)	البيت الأول (The first house)
قطة واحدة (One cat)	أول قطة (The first cat)	القطة الأولى (The first cat)
تلات بيوت (Three houses)	تالت بيت (The third house)	البيت التالت (The third house)
تلات قطط (Three cats)	تالت قطة (The third cat)	القطة التالتة (The third cat)

11 Onwards

From 11 onwards, the ordinal number is the same as the cardinal number.

There is only one way to use ordinals from 11 onwards, with the number coming after the noun and agreeing with it in gender and grammatical definiteness.

Cardinal Number	Ordinal Number (After the Noun)
تلاتة وعشرين بيت (Twenty three houses)	البيت التلاتة وعشرين (The twenty third house)
خمستاشر قطة (Fifteen cats)	القطة الخمستاشر (The fifteenth cat)

Let's have a look at these examples:
This is the third floor in the building.

ده تالت دور في العمارة.

This is the third floor in the building.

ده الدور التالت في العمارة.

This is the first train to pass today.

ده أول قطر يعدي النَّهارده.

I am in the third year in the university.

أنا في تالت سنة في الجامعة.

This is the fourth bag I buy in the same month.

دي رابع شنطة أشتريها في نفس الشهر.

I live on the sixteenth floor in this building.

أنا ساكن في الدور الستاشر في العمارة دي.

Today we will watch the twenty fifth episode.

النهارده هنشوف الحلقة الخمسة وعشرين.

Comparative and Superlative Adjectives (أفعل التَّفضيل)

The comparative and superlative forms of an adjective are formed by putting the root letters of the word into the pattern (أفعل). In Arabic, the same pattern (أفعل) is used for both the comparative and the superlative. For example, "Cairo is bigger than Dahab" (القاهرة أكبر من دهب) and "Cairo is the biggest city in Egypt" (القاهرة أكبر مدينة في مصر). Both use (أكبر) to refer to "bigger" and "the biggest."

Unlike regular adjectives, the comparative and superlative forms (أفعـل التّفضيـل) do not alter for gender or number (it has no other forms).

Exercise 3: Complete the following table.

The US is bigger than Egypt.	أمريكا أكبر من مصر.	أَكَبَر	كِبير
Michael is taller than Emad.	مايكل .... من عماد.	....	طَويل
He is the fattest guy in the class.	هو أتخن واحد في الفصل.	أَتْخَن	تِخين
Japan is further away than Iran.	اليابان .... من إيران.	....	بِعيد
Marilyn Monroe is the prettiest actress in Hollywood.	مارلين مونرو هي .... ممثّلة في هوليوود.	....	جَميل
Are the pyramids the oldest monuments in the world?	الأهرامات .... آثار في العالم؟	....	قَديم
The computer is newer than the television.	الكومبيوتر .... من التلفزيون.	....	حَديث
My fridge is full of fruits (literally, fruits are the most numerous items in my fridge).	الفاكهة هي .... حاجة في التَلاجة.	....	كِتير
Today, I am the happiest person in the world.	النَهارده أنا أسعد واحد في العالم.	أسعد	....
The turtle is the slowest animal.	السلحفة هي أبطأ حيوان.	أَبْطأ	بَطيء
Is your flat newer or is mine?	شقتك .... ولا شقتي؟	....	جِديد

English	Arabic		
I want a smaller bag, please.	عايز شنطة .... لو سمحت.	....	صُغَيَّر
She is shorter than her husband.	هي .... من جوزها.	....	قُصَيَّر
When I went on a diet, I got thinner than before.	لما عملت دايت بقيت أرفع من الأول.	أَرفَع	رُفَيَّع
Alexandria is closer than Sharm al-Sheikh.	إسكندرية .... من شرم الشَيخ.	....	قُرَيِّب
This teacher is kinder than the other one.	المدرّس ده .... من المدرّس التَّاني.	....	طَيِّب
This skirt is uglier than the last one.	الجيبة دي .... من اللي فاتت.	....	وِحش
Cairo is the most crowded city in Egypt.	القاهرة هي أزحم مدن مصر.	أَزحَم	زَحمة
Maadi is one of the spacious areas in Cairo.	المعادي من أروق المناطق في القاهرة.	أَروَق	رايِق
Today is colder than yesterday.	النهارده .... من امبارح.	أَبرَد	بارِد

If the final root letter is (و) or (ي), it will change into alif maksura (ى) for the comparative or superlative form.

Look at the following examples and complete the table:

In my opinion, the *basbousa* is better/sweeter than the cake.

في رأيي البسبوسة أحلى من الكيك.

حِلو   أَحلى

You are the richest person in the company.

إنت أغنى واحد في الشَركة.

غَني   أَغنى

This student is smarter than his friend.

الطَّالب ده .... من صاحبه.

ذَكي   ....

He is much stupider than him.

هو .... منه بكتير.

غَبي   ....

Aswan is warmer than Cairo in the winter.

أسوان .... من القاهرة في الشتا.

دافي   أَدفى

Laptops are more expensive than mobile phones.

اللاب توب .... من الموبايل.

غالي   ....

If the second and third root letters are the same, then the pattern changes slightly to the (أفعّ) form for the comparative and superlative. However, note that (جديد), whose comparative and superlative forms are (أجدد), is an exception to this rule and and follows the regular (أفعل) pattern.

Complete the following table.

What is the tastiest food in your opinion?

إيه هي .... أكلة في رأيك؟

لَذيذ   أَلَذّ

Air is lighter than water.

الهوا .... من المية

خَفيف   ....

Her work is the most important thing for her.

شغلها هو .... حاجة بالنّسبة لها.

مُهِم   أَهَم

There are fewer avocados than mangoes in Egypt.

الأفوكادو أقل من المانجا في مصر.

قَليّل   أَقَل

The adjective (كويّس) is irregular and uses (أحسن) as its comparative and superlative, thus not following any of the mentioned rules.

For example:

Coffee is better than tea for me.

القهوة أحسن من الشّاي بالنّسبالي.

أَحْسَن

(irregular comparative and superlative)

كُوَيّس

Verb Reference Table

الفعل في الماضي

Function: Past Simple

Form: الفعل الماضي

Tense: Past – Aspect: Perfective – Mood: Indicative
Something that happened in the past and is now perceived as complete.

أنا شربت قهوة إمبارح.

I drank coffee yesterday.

إنتو **رحتوا** فين الأسبوع اللي فات؟

Where *did* you *go* last week?

إنتي نمتي كام ساعة إمبارح؟

How many hours did you sleep yesterday?

البنك **اتسرق** من شهرين.

The bank *was robbed* two months ago.

أنا **مافهمتش** الدرس كويس.

I *didn't understand* the lesson well.

إحنا **اتخرجنا** السنة اللي فاتت.

We *graduated* last year.

هم **اتجوزوا** من أسبوعين.

They *got married* two weeks ago.

Function: Present Perfect

Form: اسم الفاعل

Tense/Aspect: Present perfect – Mood: Indicative – Stativity: Action or State
Something that happened in the past but which has created a state still felt
in the present, with an emphasis on the present state rather than the past
event that caused it.

أنا **صاحي** الساعة تسعة النهارده.

I *have been up* since 9 o'clock today.

إحنا واكلين من شوية.

We *have* just *eaten*.

إنت **شارب** حاجة ولا إيه؟

Have you *had* something to drink or what?

Function: Past Continuous – Action

Form: كان + المضارع مع (بـ)

Tense: Past – Aspect: Imperfective (progressive) – Mood: Indicative – Stativity: Action

An action that was ongoing when another action took place.

أنا **كنت بذاكر** إمبارح لما إنت اتصلت بيا.

I *was studying* yesterday when you called me.

كنتي بتعملي إيه لما أنا خرجت؟

What *were* you *doing* when I went out?

كنتوا بتسمعوا موسيقى لحد إمتى؟

Until what time *were* you *listening* to music?

Function: Past Continuous – State

Form: كان + اسم الفاعل

Tense: Past – Aspect: Imperfective (progressive) – Mood: Indicative – Stativity: State

A state that was ongoing when an action took place.

إنتي **كنتي فاكرة** أنا سافرت فين؟

Where *did* you *think* I traveled to?

كنا نايمين ساعة ما جيتوا لنا.

We *were asleep* when you came to us.

بابا **كان عارف** إني باخرج معاه.

Dad *knew* I was going out with him.

Function: Habitual Past

Form: كان + مضارع مع (بـ)

Tense: Past – Aspect: Imperfective (habitual) – Mood: Indicative – Stativity: Action or State

Something that regularly or repeatedly happened in the past.

كنا بنلبس بنطلون وقميص في المدرسة.

We *used to wear* trousers and shirts in school.

المصريين **كانوا بيتكلموا** قبطي زمان.

Egyptians *used to speak* Coptic in the past.

Function: Unrealized Past

Form: كان + المستقبل

Tense: Past – Mood: Conditional
An action that would have happened in the past, but didn't.

أنا **كنت هادخل** الامتحان، بس اتلغى.

I *would have taken* the exam, but it was canceled.

الناس **كانوا هيتخنقوا** جوه، لكن المطافي أنقذتهم.

The people *would have suffocated* inside, but the firemen saved them.

العربية **كانت هتخبطه**، بس وقفت في آخر لحظة.

The car *would have hit* him, but it stopped at the last minute.

البطل **كان هيعترف** لها بحبه قبل ما أبوها يدخل عليهم، بس ملحقش.

The protagonist *would have confessed* his love to her before her father came in, but he didn't get the chance.

الفعل في الزمن الحالي

Function: Present Continuous – State

Form: اسم الفاعل

Tense: Present – Aspect: Imperfective (progressive) – Mood: Indicative – Stativity: State
A state that is happening in the present.
All of us *are sitting* in the classroom now.

كلنا **قاعدين** في الفصل دلوقتي.

Do you *understand* what I'm saying?

إنت **فاهم** أنا باقول إيه؟

The teacher *is standing* and we *are sitting*.

المدرس **واقف** وإحنا **قاعدين**.

Dad is *asleep* now; who should I tell him called when he wakes up?

بابا **نايم** دلوقتي، أقول له مين لما يصحى؟

Where *are* you *living* right now?

وإنت **عايش** فين دلوقتي؟

I *am living* in Maadi, next to the metro station.

أنا **ساكن** في المعادي جنب محطة المترو.

Function: Present Continuous – Action

Form: المضارع مع (ب)

Tense: Present – Aspect: Imperfective (progressive) – Mood: Indicative – Stativity: Action

An action that is happening in the present
I *am reading* the newspaper on the balcony.

أنا **باقرا** الجورنان في البلكونة.

We *are watching* a movie right now.

إحنا **بنتفرج** على فيلم دلوقتي.

What *are* you *eating* now?

إنتو **بتاكلوا** إيه دلوقتي؟

Function: Habitual Present

Form: المضارع مع (ب)

Tense: Present – Aspect: Imperfective (habitual) – Mood: Indicative – Stativity: Action or State

Something that regularly or repeatedly happens
I *go* to school every day by metro.

أنا **باروح** المدرسة كل يوم بالمترو.

The sun *rises* after 6am these days.

الشمس **بتطلع** اليومين دول بعد الساعة ٦.

What time is the sunset *call* to prayer?

هو المغرب **بيدّن** الساعة كام؟

Where *does* your daughter *play* tennis?

بنتك **بتلعب** تنس فين؟

I *like* oranges a lot.

أنا **باحب** البرتقان قوي.

Arabs *speak* in different dialects.

العرب **بيتكلموا** لهجات مختلفة.

Why *do* you only *drink* mineral water?

ليه **بتشربوا** مية معدنية بس؟

Ostriches and penguins *can't fly*.

النعام والبطاريق **مابتطيرش**.

Function: Future

Forms:

(i) المستقبل

or

(ii) اسم الفاعل

Tense: Future – Mood: Indicative
Something that will happen in the future.
Form: المستقبل
What *will* you *be doing* tomorrow?

إنتو بكرة **هتعملوا** إيه؟

We *will play* a match against the other school.

إحنا **هنلعب** ماتش مع المدرسة التانية.

There *will be* a really good film on TV this Friday.

التلفزيون **هيجيب** فيلم حلو قوي يوم الجمعة.

Form (for movement verbs only): اسم الفاعل
When *will* you *be going* to the cinema?

إنتو **رايحين** السينما إمتى؟

Are you *leaving* today?

إنتي **ماشية** النهارده؟

We *are traveling* tomorrow.

إحنا خلاص **مسافرين** بكرة.

الفعل في الصّيغة الافتراضيّة

Function: Subjunctive

Forms:

(i) (المضارع من غير (بـ))
or
(ii) (اسم الفاعل + المضارع من غير (بـ))
or
(iii) (المضارع مع (بـ) + المضارع من غير (بـ))

Mood: Subjunctive

Events that may, could, or should happen.

The idea of the verb rather than a specific instance of it.

Form: المضارع من غير (بـ)

We want *to go* somewhere tomorrow to have some fun.

عايزين **نروح** بكرة أي مكان نتفسح فيه.

Can you *come* see me next Tuesday?

إنت ممكن **تيجي** لي يوم التلات الجاي؟

Shall I *open* the window or are you cold?

أفتح الشباك ولا إنت بردان؟

Would you *like* to have a language exchange activity together?

تحب نعمل تبادل لغوي مع بعض؟

I *would lik*e to eat fish.

نفسي **آكل** سمك.

Form: اسم الفاعل + المضارع من غير (بـ)

I *want to listen* to music.

عايزة أسمع موسيقى.

Form: المضارع مع (بـ) + المضارع من غير (بـ)

I *love eating* fish.

باحب آكل سمك.

The Conditional

There are two kinds of conditionals in Arabic: the conditional for events that can still happen—for example, "If I go to the cinema tonight," or "لـو رحت سـينما بالليل"—and the conditional for events that are impossible or can no longer happen—for example, "If I were born in Japan," or "لو (كنت) اتولدت فـي اليابان."

Conditions that Can Happen

A conditional sentence consists of two clauses: a conditional clause that declares a condition—e.g., "if you ask nicely," or "لـو طلبـت بـأدب"—and a re-sultant clause that states what will happen if the condition is fulfilled—e.g., "I will give you my cake," or "هادّيـك الكيـك بتاعـي."

There are a few different ways of expressing this conditional in Arabic.

For the conditional clause you can either use:

- (لو) plus a verb in whatever tense you would normally use it to describe the action (i.e., the tense it takes place in), or

- (إن، لو، إذا) and the past tense.

Note, however, that if you want to talk about a regular or repeated action happening in the present tense with (بِ), you can only use the first option. As for the resultant clause, you can use either:

- the future, or
- the imperative (if you want to give an order).

If you take this exam, you will pass.

لو دخلت الامتحان ده هتنجح.

If you go to Egypt, you will learn Arabic well.

لو رحت مصر هتتعلم عربي كويس.

If you finish the book, bring it along!

لو خلصت الكتاب هاته.

If you like fruit, eat a lot of it!

لو بتحب الفاكهة كلها كتير.

If he watches American movies regularly, he'll learn English easily.

لو بيشوف أفلام أمريكية كتير هيتعلم إنجليزي بسهولة.

If you go to Spain, tell me so that I can come with you!

لو هتروح إسبانيا قول لي عشان آجي معاك.

If they win the match, they will get a prize.

إن فازوا في الماتش هياخدوا جايزة.

If you pass the exam, I will buy you a car.

إن نجحت في الامتحان هاجيب لك عربية.

If you love her that much, marry her!

إذا كنت بتحبها قوي كده اتجوزها.

If you take the medicine as prescribed, you will get better in a couple of days.

إذا خدت الدوا في معاده هتكون كويس خلال يومين.

Conditions that Can't Happen

If you want to describe a condition that is impossible or can no longer be fulfilled because it is in the past, then for the conditional clause you can either use:

- (لو) plus a verb in whatever tense you would normally use it, or
- (إن، لو، إذا) plus (كان) plus a verb in whatever tense you would normally use it, or
- the past tense.

Note, however, that if you want to talk about a regular or repeated action happening in the present tense with (بـ), you can only use the first or second option, but not the past tense.

As for the resultant clause, you can either use:

- كان + the past, or
- كان + the future, or
- كان + the present (formal).

Note that the future and the past in the resultant clause both convey the same meaning while the present is more formal and poetic.

If I were a bird, I would fly.

لو كنت طير كنت هاطير.

If I were Italian, I would have lived in Rome my whole life.

لو كنت إيطالي كنت عشت في روما طول حياتي.

If I spoke Russian, I would have gone to Russia.

لو (كنت) باتكلم روسي كنت رحت روسيا.

If I worked as a lawyer, I would have earned more than I earn now.

لو (كنت) اشتغلت محامي كنت كسبت أكتر من دلوقتي.

If I had been born in the United States, I would have gotten the American citizenship.

لو (كنت) اتولدت في أمريكا كنت خدت الجنسية الأمريكية.

If I were not afraid of water, I would have swum.

لو مش/ماكنتش باخاف من المية كنت أعوم.

English Translation of the Songs

1. The Forbidden

What is forbidden is the sin itself, my lying friend.
I am not forbidden to sing.
I am not forbidden to love.
What is forbidden is to speak half-truths.
I am not forbidden to make art.
I am not forbidden to feel.
What is forbidden is to speak half-truths.

2. Light of My Eye

My darling, the light of my eye, you who dwell in my imagination,
I've adored you for many years, without anyone else occupying my mind.
My darling, my darling, my darling, the light of my eye,
You who dwell in my imagination.
I have seen the prettiest eyes in the universe.
My God, how charming yours are!
Your eyes are with me . . . your eyes are enough.
They light my nights.
My darling, my darling, my darling, the light of my eye,
You who dwell in my imagination.
Your heart called out to me and said that you love me.
My God, how you have calmed me!
The beginning is with you, but so is the whole story.

I'm with you till the end.
My darling, my darling, my darling, the light of my eye.

3. I Have Loved

I have loved her but I am done, so why the blame?
Would she like that I say "I wish this love would leave me?"
Since I have settled for her leaving me, let them say what they want to say.
My love and I adore each other in a way that doesn't exist elsewhere, not even in dreams.
I love her even when we fight, and, hear me, her absence is a curse!
Since I have settled for her leaving me, I am not angry at the world.

4. Life Is Sweet like Sugar

Lovely! How the world is lovely!
Live now and tell me you love me.
Lovely! How the world is lovely!
Live now and tell me you love me.
One night . . . let us live for one night.
Kiss me and hold me so tight.
Sugar! I swear to God, life is sugar!
Stay up and love life more.
Sugar! I swear to God, life is sugar!
Stay up and love life more.
One night . . . enjoy yourself even if just for one night.
Live for one night because life is beautiful like sugar.
Lovely! How the world is lovely!
Live now and tell me you love me.
Lovely! How the world is lovely!
Live now and tell me you love me.
One night . . . let us live for one night.
Kiss me and hold me so tight.
How much we have sacrificed! How much!
And what have we ever gained from the words "how much"
Except for blame, censure, and rebuke,
Except for pain, torture, and regret?
I'll enjoy myself even if just for one night.
Live for one night because life is beautiful like sugar.

5. Our Great Love

Our great love—the first and last love!
You who embrace us under your shade and your plentiful resources.
You, the one who is loved by our beloved ones, both present and absent.
We are millions, but in your love all of us are family and relatives.
Your word brings us together . . . your revolution motivates us.
Our joy is your joy and our victory is your victory.
And on your festivals and celebrations, we congratulate you and sing your anthem.
Live and be safe . . . live and be safe . . . live and be safe, my homeland.

6. Remember Me!

Remember me!
You who have captured me through your beauty and your eyes.
Remember me!
And if your heart ever felt my heart then visit me!
In my eyes, you're all that I have,
The joy of my youth, and this entire world.
The first time I saw you,
You touched my heart and, in a single glance, I forgot its wounds.
I found you, the most beautiful love story, and I forgot those who are no longer with me.
Don't leave me all alone,
And let your heart come to me again if I call you.
What we have is all the love in the world, and life with you passes in seconds.
In my eyes, you're all that I have,
The joy of my youth, and this entire world.
Remember me!
You who have captured me through your beauty and your eyes.
In my eyes, you're all that I have,
The joy of my youth, and this entire world.
Remember me!

7. I Adore the Sea

I adore the sea.
It's affectionate like you, my darling, and sometimes, like you, it's crazy and
it moves away.
And sometimes it's confused like you, sometimes sad like you,
sometimes full of patience.
I adore the sea.
I adore the sky
because it's forgiving like you, full of stars and joy,
beloved yet strange,
and because it's distant but sometimes near, just like you,
with melodious eyes.
I adore the sky.
I adore the road,
because our meetings, our joy, and our suffering occur on it.
Our friends and our younger years were on it.
Our tears laughed on it and our candles cried on it.
And we lost our friends on it.
I adore the road.
I adore the sea, I adore the sky, and I adore the road.
Because they are life, and you, my darling, you are my whole life.

8. This Is What Happened

This is what happened,
you don't have the right to blame me.
How can you blame me, my friend,
when the resources of our country aren't in our hands?
First give me useful advice and then blame me all you want.
Egypt, mother of all things odd,
your people are noble but the enemy rebukes them.
Look after those who love you, for they are the true supporters of the cause
(i.e., independence).
Rather than letting the envious rejoice at our misfortune
give me your hand and let us strive together.
Let us unite so that our hands would be strong.

9. The World Is a Feather in the Air

Choir: The world is a feather in the air that flies without wings.
Today we are together but where will we be tomorrow?
In the world . . . in the world.
Singer: How often people have met without prior arrangements!
And how often people have begged for separation to keep its distance!
Choir: Whose hands brought them together only for them to separate around him?
Singer: Why did they meet?
Choir: Why?
Singer: And why did they separate?
Choir: Why?
The world is a feather in the air that flies without wings.
Today we are together but where will we be tomorrow?
In the world . . . in the world.
Singer: To those who ask about life, just take it as it comes,
with its smiles, with its cries, with its grief, with its affection.
Choir: How often people complain about life!
Singer: Yet how many are also satisfied with it!
Choir: Ah!
Singer: And how many suffer from it!
Choir: Ah!
The world is a feather in the air that flies without wings.
Today we are together but where will we be tomorrow?
In the world . . . in the world.

10. He Scribbled

He scribbled and made a mess. He drew on the wall with colored pencils.
What should I do with you, Hamada? What you did is the worst habit.
If you want to draw, draw, but without scribbling on the walls.
He scribbled and made a mess. He drew on the wall with colored pencils.
Draw a tree, the Nile, and seas, but draw on the board.
Tomorrow you'll be a famous artist
and we'll want to take pictures with you.
Dream of becoming like Picasso. He too was once a child and he too wished, but he didn't scribble on walls.

He scribbled and made a mess. He drew on the wall with colored pencils.
Draw and dream of the future; those who dream will get what they want eventually.
What's ahead of you is better.
Every hobby has its rules.
Hold your pen, your colors, and your brush, and draw with them
but on your canvas.
Why would you draw on the wall?
He scribbled and made a mess. He drew on the wall with colored pencils.

11. Oh, How Charming Your Eyes Are!

Oh, how charming your eyes are! Oh, how beautiful your eyelashes are!
I forgot about the nights you've illuminated for me. Oh, how I have forgotten!
Your compassion lasts days while your harshness lasts years.
Sometimes you are careless, and you forget me.
Sometimes you are affectionate and sometimes you are harsh.
I do not know what is wrong with you!
If only your personality was as beautiful as your looks
then you would be even more beautiful and our love would grow even stronger.
Oh, how charming your eyes are! Oh, how beautiful your eyelashes are!
I forgot about the nights you've illuminated for me. Oh, how I have forgotten!
You forget the sweetness of the nights we spent together even though the roses still hold your fragrance.
I kept on watering them with my tears,
and I let the fire of my longing keep them warm.
You have been far from me for so long,
and I have been alone since.
I wonder if you are alone too. Come to me and let's be together.
Oh, how charming your eyes are! Oh, how beautiful your eyelashes are!
I forgot about the nights you've illuminated for me. Oh, how I have forgotten!

12. OK Dice

Fine, dice. Yes, dice.
Do you like playing like this, dice?
We stay up together at night and we play together.
You make us happy for a day but then cry for a month.
You break up with us for a day but then get back together with us for a month.
Do you like that, dice? As you like, dice.
You pretend to be a lamb but you're a ghoul.
I am the camel, and you are the burden.
Show me my fortune,
or will you refrain because of my patience?
Fine, dice. Yes, dice.
You have a thousand faces, a thousand eyes,
and a thousand changing laughs.
I'm following you but where are you taking me?
Are you just teasing or are you ordering me?
Fine, dice. Yes, dice.

13. My Beautiful Mom

Oh mom! You're so beautiful . . . you're the sweetest song!
You live in my heart and inside my being.
You are so dear to me . . . you are the light of my eyes.
You were my first word.
Mom, mom, mom, oh mom!
You're an angel from heaven, mom.
Under your wing, I live and I am happy.
You are my life and my smiles.
You are my hopes and my happiness.
Who raised me, who? And who made me happy, who?
It's only you . . . oh my beautiful mom!
Mom, mom, mom, oh mom!
When I hug you and you hug me back,
the world cannot contain my happiness,
my longing builds up, and I find myself yearning
to hug you again.

Who raised me, who? And who made me happy, who?
It's only you . . . oh my beautiful mom!
Mom, mom, mom, oh mom!
Even if I traveled the whole world on a daily basis,
I wouldn't find anyone like you in this world!
The happiest moment in my whole life
is when I see you before me, mom.
Who raised me, who? And who made me happy, who?
It's only you . . . oh my beautiful mom!
Mom, mom, mom, oh mom!

14. Where's the Truth?

Where's the truth, uncle?
Our hearts are weary from searching for it.
It changes every moment just like sunrise and sunset.
And what is in our hearts, uncle? Our hearts are full of questions.
Some hearts are empty, having neither goodness nor evil.
Some hearts are too keen to injure and hurt.
And those with pure little warm hearts have bitter tongues.
How bitter the question is for those who struggled in life!
So what should we do? We should open the doors of our hearts.
How amazing you are, uncle! You can open the doors of our imagination.
Some hearts are wandering, and you don't know their secrets.
They stretch their wings in search of land.
And those with pure little warm hearts have bitter tongues.

15. Salma ya Salama

Across the wide world and its many countries
I traveled, traveled, traveled.
And when my first love called me
I left everything and came, came,
and threw myself into his embrace and sang:
Salma ya salama, we left and returned safe and sound.
Our love is still pure,
and the weather is still warm.
The moon is still there.

And after the sun sets, we all get together in a boat,
and stay up all night,
chatting and singing together:
Salma ya salama, we left and returned safe and sound.
There is a tree in a garden that has a sign.
I used to think about it so often and wonder whether it was still there and
whether my heart was still carved on it.
Yes, it is still there and my heart is still carved on it!
Salma ya salama, we left and returned safe and sound.

16. It's Spring Now!

It's spring now and the weather is wonderful
so stop talking about anything else!
Stop! Stop! Stop! Stop!
We will not discuss this.
No arguing. It is spring now.
It is spring. It is spring.
The bare trees are blossoming. Oh my God!
The birds are now playful and careless. Really?
So when will we allow ourselves to rejoice?
Now or in September?
You know what they say:
Don't postpone today's joy to tomorrow,
and if we catch someone who is worried, we will be truly upset with them.
Let's play a game. Let's have a competition to see who has the purest laugh-
ter.
The funny ones will of course win, not the serious ones.
The roses are blossoming; look at them. They are dancing and covering
their shyness.
If you love the prophet (i.e., if you have faith), brothers, clap your hands to
the rhythm.
You know what they say:
Locals prescribe the sun and fresh air by waterbodies for health and a long
life,
without having to worry about medicine, illness, or bitterness.

17. The Best People

Let's chat; what else have we to do?

We are chatting and rejoicing; what else have we to do?

We would like to get to know each other; what else have we to do? It would be an honor for us to know you; what else have we to do?

So where are you from, our fellow citizen, and what is your original town? The best people!

Sohag, city of mawwals, Sohag, city of pigeon towers,

Sohag, my friend, is the bride of the Nile.

Sohag, my father, is the city of hardworking people who easily earn money because they are serious, strong, and responsible, our fellow citizens.

On the bridge of Banha, my sweetheart,

the handkerchief of my love made me blink,

for after the separation and the longing, love has brought us together again, on the bridge of Banha . . . on the bridge of Banha.

O Ismailia! O Ismailia! I like to visit you at sunset

so that my friends and I could ride a felucca and sing to the tunes of the *simsimiya*.

Ah, la la la, my love, la la la, my soul, la la la

How do we go to Mahalla, O man from Samanud? How do we go to Mahalla, the land of my ancestors?

How do we go to Mahalla, the famous city? How do we go to Mahalla, O man from Samanud?

The best people are in Alexandria, the swaggering city by the sea.

From Sidi Bishr to Abu al-Abbas, what a beautiful view!

How beautiful the port is, which swings our longing,

and with three hundred thousand ships passing and honking!

Narazan, the town of reliable and brave men, the town of brides and grooms.

May God protect you from humans and jinns, sweet town clothed in green.

As for me, I am from Shubra in Cairo and I am related to its sweet residents.

They are beautiful and charming, with brown eyes and wearing necklaces made from jasmine.

And the Nile is laughing and singing, remembering me and asking about me.

I go to it and find it waiting with the best people.

The best people!

18. Mint Seller

O mint seller, fragrant with a minty smell,
bring a present to the flirty woman who made my heart burn, enjoying its
torture.
When I ask her to meet, she declines.
Mint seller, fragrant with a minty smell.
She is the light of my eye. Only she is in my heart.
Although she tires me, she still pleases me. What can I do?
Sugar seller, sweet man,
I think of my sweetheart day and night.
Her absence got long and I can endure it no more.
But when I ask her to meet, she ignores me.
Sesame seller, handsome man,
her body is beautiful and proportionate
When I smell her sweet scent, life smiles to my face,
but when I ask her to meet, she fakes stories.
O mint seller, fragrant with a minty smell,
bring a present to the flirty woman.
Sugar seller, sweet man,
I think of my sweetheart day and night.

19. We Want Dad

Why weren't you our dad? You would have stayed with us forever.
We would have seen you all day, from morning to night.
Why don't you always stay with us? We want a father to be with us.
We want a father to be with us and we wish you were both our dad and
teacher.
We don't have a dad but we want one and you are dad to us.
You teach us how to love and you give us the best gifts.
You even easily explain to us the words we find difficult.
Why don't you always stay with us? We want a father to be with us.
We want a father to be with us and we wish you were both our dad and
teacher.
You are like a father to us and more. You are kind to us too.
You are the song we sing and the love that warms us.
You made us love life, which became full of flowers.

Why don't you always stay with us? We want a father to be with us.

We want a father to be with us and we wish you were both our dad and teacher.

With you, life became beautiful and we learned what love is.

We used to see you before you arrived and you used to see us from where you were.

Even if you went far away and were absent during our lesson time, we would still wait for you.

Why don't you always stay with us? We want a father to be with us.

We want a father to be with us and we wish you were both our dad and teacher.

20. How?

My love, how could you accept that I love even your name while you keep increasing my confusion without even feeling for my kindheartedness? How?

I can't find any motivation to adore you and my sincerity in loving you does not intervene.

How could you keep bending my head when all I've done is raise yours? How?

I am your oldest street and your hopes during hard times.

I am a child that clung to you in the middle of the way but you misled him.

If I had a choice in loving you, my heart would have changed by now.

But I swear by your life, I will keep changing you until you accept me.

My love, how could you accept that I love even your name while you keep increasing my confusion without even feeling for my kindheartedness? How?

I can't find any motivation to adore you and my sincerity in loving you does not intervene.

How could you keep bending my head when all I've done is raise yours? How?

How could you leave me during my weakness? Why aren't you by my side when all of my life I have made sure not to glance fear in your eyes?

How can I have your back on land and in sea when I spend the nights with a bent and bare back?

I am your oldest street and your hopes during hard times.

I am a child that clung to you in the middle of the way but you misled him.

If I had a choice in loving you, my heart would have changed by now.

But I swear by your life, I will keep changing you until you accept me.

My love, how could you accept that I love even your name while you keep increasing my confusion without even feeling for my kindheartedness? How?

I can't find any motivation to adore you and my sincerity in loving you does not intervene.

How could you keep bending my head when all I've done is raise yours? How?

سير المطربين والملحنين والشعراء

أحمد شتا

شاعر مصري اتولد في الإسكندرية سنة ١٩٦٢. التحق بكلية الحقوق بجامعة الإسكندرية واشتغل محامي ٣ سنين. كان بيحب اللغة العربية، وبدأ يكتب الشعر وهو عنده ١٣ سنة في يوم وفاة عبد الحليم حافظ. من أشهر أعماله أغنية "هاوري لك" و"آه باحبك يا حبيبي" لسميرة سعيد، و"هاسهرك" لوردة، و"أحلى ما فيكي" لهشام عباس، و"نور العين" لعمرو دياب، و"فاكرك يا ناسيني" لمحمد فؤاد، و"توأم روحي" و"مغرم يا ليل" و"فرق كبير" و"سيدتي الجميلة" لراغب علامة، و"كلام الناس" لجورج وسوف.

أحمد فرحات

ملحن وموزع مصري. قدم أغاني كتير من كلمات الشاعر نصر الدين ناجي زي "كان فاضل" و"طعم البيوت" و"إزاي" لمحمد منير. ومن أعماله أغنيات "براجع نفسي" لشرين عبد الوهاب و"خليك فاكر" لبهاء سلطان.

أم كلثوم

أشهر مطربة مصرية وعربية. اسمها الأصلي فاطمة إبراهيم البلتاجي. لُقّبت بـ"كوكب الشرق." اتولدت في الدقهلية في ديسمبر ١٩٠٤. تُمثّل قمّة الغناء المصري طول القرن العشرين. مثّلت في أكتر من فيلم، زي فيلم "سلامة" وشاركت بصوتها بس في فيلم "رابعة العدويّة."
غير الأغاني الرُومانسيّة والدّينيّة اللي غنّتها، غنّت كمان أناشيد وأغاني وطنيّة كتيرة زي "منصورة يا ثورة أحرار" و"فرحة القنال" و "والله زمان يا سلاحي" وغنّت "طوف وشوف" قدّام جمال عبد النّاصر. واتبرّعت بحفلات عملتها في باريس وفي أماكن تانية للمساهمة في المجهود الحربي بعد حرب ١٩٦٧. كرّمتها الحكومة المصريّة وإدّتها جايزة الدّولة التّقديريّة. من أغانيها المشهورة "أمل حياتي" و"إنت الحب" و"أغدًا ألقاك" و"هجرتك" و"الحب كله."
وفي ٣ فبراير سنة ١٩٧٥ انتقلت أم كلثوم إلى الرفيق الأعلى، وخرج ملايين المصريين يودّعوها في جنازة من أكبر الجنازات اللي شافتها مصر.

بخيت بيومي

شاعر مصري اتولد سنة ١٩٣٧. حفظ القرآن وهو صغير وحصل على الثانوية الأزهرية سنة ١٩٦٠ ودبلوم الخطوط، وتخصص في النسيج والزخرفة سنة ١٩٦١. انتقل للقاهرة واشتغل مدرس في مدرسة خاصة وبعدين خطاط في القلعة. سنة ١٩٦٩ غنت ليلى مراد من أعماله وبعد كده صباح وسعاد محمد ووردة ومحمد عبد المطلب. كتب بعض المسلسلات الإذاعية زي "سها هانم" لفؤاد المهندس. وكتب فوازير الإذاعة لآمال فهمي لمدة ١٣ سنة.

بديع خيري

مؤلف مصري مشهور. اتولد سنة ١٨٩٣ وتوفي سنة ١٩٦٦. كان بيحب الأدب والفن وكتب الشعر ونشر بعض أعماله الأولى في الجرايد. وكمان كان بيحب المسرح فكان بيروح مسارح سلامة حجازي وعبد الرحمن رشدي وجورج أبيض، وكوّن نادي للتمثيل مع أصحابه. قدم مع الملحن الكبير سيد درويش والممثل المشهور نجيب الريحاني مسرحيات غنائية تضم تابلوهات كتير بتتكلم عن مشكلات المجتمع المختلفة. كتب بديع أغنيات أوبريت "العشرة الطيبة" لكن نص المسرحية كان ترجمة عن الفرنسية لمحمد تيمور. بعد كده كتب تابلوهات الطوائف الصناعية والعمال والموظفين زي "الحلوة دي قامت تعجن." وغير المسرح كتب "قوم يا مصري" وأغنيات وطنية كتيرة.

بليغ حمدي

اتولد في القاهرة في ٧ أكتوبر سنة ١٩٣٢. وهو الابن الأخير لأب متخصص في علم البصريات بيشتغل مدرس علوم ويجيد العزف على البيانو وأم مثقفة اتعلّم منها الأغاني الشعبيّة. إخواته هم صفيّة وأسماء ودكتور مرسي سعد الدين وحسام. كان بليغ الوحيد في العيلة اللي احترف الموسيقى. أتقن العزف على العود وهو عمره ٩ سنين بس. درس في كلية الحقوق في جامعة فؤاد الأول (جامعة القاهرة حاليًا)، لكنه وقف لحد لحد سنة تالتة لانشغاله بالموسيقى. درس الموسيقى بشكل أكاديمي في معهد فؤاد الأول (معهد الموسيقى العربيّة دلوقتي). درس نظريات الموسيقى على يد مدرّس اسمه ميناتو ودرس البيانو على يد مدرسة اسمها جوليا وكان للدراسة دي أثر كبير في حياته الفنيّة بعد كده. لحّن أغاني لكبار المطربين والمطربات في عصره زي أم كلثوم، وعبد الحليم حافظ، وشادية، ووردة، وصباح، ونجاة وغيرهم، وبيقى واحد من أشهر وأهم الملحنين في القرن العشرين.

عمل الموسيقى التصويريّة لأفلام ومسرحيّات ومسلسلات تلفزيونيّة وإذاعيّة كتير زي "شيء من الخوف" و"العمر لحظة" ومسرحية "زقاق المدق" ومسلسل "بوّابة الحلواني." توفي بليغ في ١٢ سبتمبر ١٩٩٣ عن عمر يناهز ٦٢ سنة بعد صراع طويل مع مرض الكبد، وكان يوم وفاته موافق لذكرى رحيل الموسيقار سيد درويش عام ١٩٢٣. ووصفه "الأهرام" في اليوم التّالي لوفاته بقوله "مات ملك الموسيقى."

جيف برنيف

ملحن أغنية "سالمة يا سلامة" لداليدا.

داليدا

فنّانة ومغنيّة إيطاليّة مصريّة. اتولدت في يناير ١٩٣٣ في القاهرة لأبوين إيطاليين مهاجرين. بدأت حياتها بالمشاركة في مسابقة ملكة جمال مصر وفازت بيها سنة ١٩٤٥. بدأت حياتها الفنيّة في فرنسا وغنّت بلغات كتير زي العربي والإيطالي والعبري والفرنساوي واليوناني والإنجليزي والإسباني والألماني. في سنة ١٩٨٦ شاركت في الفيلم المصري "اليوم السّادس" من إخراج يوسف شاهين، والفيلم نجح بشكل كبير. في سنة ١٩٨٧ رحلت منتحرة بتناول جرعة زائدة من الأقراص المهدئة، وادَفَنت في باريس.

دينا الوديدي

مطربة مصرية شابة لها طابع خاص في أداءها بيميزها عن غيرها. كانت بدايتها مع الغنى سنة ٢٠٠٨ من خلال فرقة الورشة. وأسست فرقتها الخاصة سنة ٢٠١١. قدمت كذا تجربة مع مجموعة من الموسيقيين زي فتحي سلامة وهاني عادل وفرقة مسار إجباري.

رياض السنباطي

موسيقار مصريّ مشهور. اتولد سنة ١٩٠٦ بفارسكور وعاش طفولته وصباه في مدينة المنصورة. كان والده مغني وملحّن. درس رياض في المدرسة لكنه كان بيهرب منها لحضور مجالس الغناء. حفّظه والده بعض الموشّحات والأدوار وكان بيصحبه في الأفراح. اتعلّم العزف وسمعه سيد درويش سنة ١٩٢٢ وطلب من والده إنه يتبناه لكن والده رفض. راح القاهرة في أواخر العشرينيات والتحق بمعهد الموسيقى العربيّة وبدل أن يلتحق به كطالب عيّنوه مدرس للعود لبراعته في العزف.

لحّن للمسرح "سهرة بريئة" لفرقة منيرة المهديّة وبعد كده "عروس الشّرق" و"آدم وحواء" لنفس الفرقة، ولحن كمان فصل من أوبريت "سميراميس." اختارته أم كلثوم إنه يكون ملحّنها التالت مع القصبجي وزكريا أحمد سنة ١٩٣٦، وكان أول ألحانه لها مونولوج "النّوم." ولحّن ٥٧٥ لحنًا تقدر تقول بثقة عنها كلها إنها جميلة، منها ٣٠٢ لأم كلثوم لوحدها، و٢٠ لنور الهدى، و٢٧ لحن لعبد الغنيّ السّيد، و٢٩ لحن لليلى مراد، و٢٥ لحن لسعاد محمد، و١٢ لحن لنجاة، وغنّى ٨٢ لحن بصوته. وبلغ القمّة في تلحين القصائد، وعدد معزوفاته حوالي ٣٠ قطعة منها "لونجا رياض،" و"رقصة شنغهاي،" و"ليلة البدر،" و"القبلة الأولى."

قام ببطولة فيلم واحد هو "حبيب قلبي" مع هدى سلطان، وظهر في لقطة واحدة في فيلم محمد عبد الوهاب "الوردة البيضاء" عام ١٩٣٣.

حصل على جائزة الدّولة التّقديريّة عام ١٩٧٧، ووسام الفنون والعلوم من الطبقة الأولى، وحصل على الدكتوراة الفخرية من أكاديمية الفنون عام ١٩٧٧.

من أشهر أعماله "أراك عصي الدمع،" و"أروح لمين،" و"أقبل الليل،" و"إله الكون،" و"عرفت الهوى،" و"رباعيات الخيام،" و"صوت الوطن،" و"دليلي احتار" و"هلت ليالي القمر،" و"إن كنت ناسي،" و"يا هاجر بحبك،" و"يا حبنا الكبير،" و"أنا النّيل مقبرة للغزاة،" و"يا حبيب الروح،" و"ولد الهدى،" و"حديث الروح." توفي في ٧ سبتمبر سنة ١٩٨١.

ريما خشيش

مطربـة لبنانيّة. اتولدت سنة ١٩٧٤ في الخيام بجنوب لبنان. والدها كامل خشيش عازف قانون. بدأت الغناء في طفولتها. وهي عندها ٩ سنين كانت عضوة في فرقة "بيروت للتّراث." درست الموسيقى العربيّة الكلاسيكيّة في المعهد الوطنيّ العالي للموسيقى (الكونسيرفتوار) في بيروت. كانت عضوة في فرقة هولنديّة عراقيّة لبنانيّة باسم "قطار الشرق." أصدرت مع الفرقة ألبوم غنائي باسم الفرقة سنة ٢٠٠٢، وبعدها بدأت الغناء المنفرد فأصدرت ألبومَي "ياللي" سنة ٢٠٠٦ و"فلك" سنة ٢٠٠٩.
تمتاز بأسلوبها اللي بيمزج بين الأغاني العربيّة القديمة وموسيقى الجاز. وقد اعتبرها النّقاد مغنّية المثقفين ومطربتهم المميّزة اللي بترفض الغنى في المطاعم والحانات والمقاهي واللي بترفض حصر جمهورها المتذوّق لإيقاعات الطّرب الأصيل بكبار السن، لكن تذوق غناء ريما وطربها بيجذب شرائح اجتماعيّة متنوعة من جميع الأعمار والانتماءات.

سعاد حسني

فنّانة مصريّة راحلة. اتولدت في القاهرة في يناير ١٩٤٣. وهي أخت الفنّانة نجاة. لُقّبت بلقب "سندريلا الشّاشة العربيّة." كان صاحب الفضل في اكتشاف موهبتها الفنيّة الشّاعر عبد الرّحمن الخميسي، وكان أول أفلامها "حسن ونعيمة" إنتاج سنة ١٩٥٨. شاركت في حوالي ٨٢ فيلم كان من أشهرها "صغيرة على الحب" و"الكرنك" و"شفيقة ومتولي" و"أميرة حبّي أنا" و"المتوحّشة." اتجوزت أكثر من مرة فكان من أزواجها علي بدرخان وزكي فطين عبد الوهاب. حصلت على جوائز كتير، وشهادة تقدير من الرئيس الراحل أنور السّادات في عيد الفنّ سنة ١٩٧٩. تُوفيت نتيجة سقوطها من بلكونة شقّتها في حادث غامض في لندن في يونيو ٢٠٠١.

سعد عبد الوهاب

مطرب وملحن مصري معروف. اتولد سنة ١٩٢٩ وعاش طفولته وشبابه مع عمه الموسيقار الكبير محمد عبد الوهاب في بيت العيلة. اتخرج من كلية الزراعة جامعة القاهرة سنة ١٩٤٩. اشتغل مذيع في الإذاعة لمدة ٥ سنين، وفي نفس الوقت لحن أغنية من كلمات زميل دراسته الشاعر أحمد شفيق كامل. شارك في بعض الأفلام المصرية زي "العيش والملح" سنة ١٩٤٩ و"أماني العمر" و"بلدي وخفة" وآخرها "علموني الحب" سنة ١٩٥٧.
التحق بالكونسيرفتوار مع عدد من الملحنين ودرس فيه لمدة ٣ سنين. ومن أشهر أغانيه "قلبي القاسي" و"اليومين دول قلبه ماله" و"الدنيا ريشة في هوا" و"فين جنة أحلامي." توفي في ٢٢ نوفمبر ٢٠٠٤.

سمير حبيب

موسيقار وملحن وموزع بارع. أسس في فترة السبعينات الفرقة الغنائية الجيتس (The Jets) ولحن أغلب أغانيها. ومن أعماله المشهورة لفرقة الجيتس "سيدي يا سيدي" و"طلب قهوة وماشربهاش" و"فطومة" و"ليندا ليندا." من أشهر ألحانه أغنية "أحسن ناس" لداليدا. تخصص في تلحين الفوازير لنيللي وشريهان وسمير غانم، وهو مبتكر شخصية "فطوطة." وكمان ساعد في تصمير روائع الأعمال

الكرتونية لوالت ديزني العالمية. كان بيصمم الإعلانات التلفزيونية وبيملك ويدير أستوديو إكو ساوند (Eko Sound Productions) اللي سجل فيه أغلب المطربين أعمالهم زي محمد منير وعمرو دياب.

سمير صبري

ممثل ومغني اتولد في الإسكندرية سنة ١٩٣٢. اتعلم في مدرسة "فيكتوريا" وكان بيحب السينما والمسرح ومثل في أكتر من ١٠٠ فيلم. أول أفلامه كان "اللص والكلاب" سنة ١٩٦٢. تخصص في إعادة أغاني محمد فوزي ومحمد عبد الوهاب. قدم بعض البرامج للأطفال والكبار أشهرها "هذا المساء." من أشهر أغانيه "اضحك يا أبو علي."

سيد درويش

مطرب وملحن مصري. اتولد في كوم الدكة في إسكندرية سنة ١٨٩٢. هو في نظر نقاد كتير رائد الموسيقى العربية الحديثة. و تقريبا كل اللي جم بعده اتأثروا بيه، وعلى رأسهم موسيقار الأجيال محمد عبد الوهاب اللي دايما بيأكد على الحقيقة دي. كان بيحيي الحفلات لأصحابه في إسكندرية فاشتهر في المدينة في مجال الغناء واشتغل فترة عامل بناء وكان بيغني لهم بجانب تجويده للقرآن. اتعرف على فرقة "سليم عطا الله" التمثيلية وسافر معاهم للشام سنة ١٩٠٩ و١٩١٢ ودرس هناك الموسيقى العربية على إيد عثمان الموصلي. وبعد رجوعه من رحلته الأخيرة من الشام اتجه للتلحين. راح القاهرة وعاش فيها من سنة ١٩١٧ بعد شهرة أغنيته العظيمة "زوروني كل سنة مرة." شارك في ثورة ١٩١٩ بأغنيته "قوم يا مصري."
واشتهر كملحن لأغاني وموسيقا المسرحيات الغنائية ومنها "فيروز شاه" و"ولو" و"فشر" و"العشرة الطيبة" و"راحت عليك."
من أشهر أعماله الغنائية أغاني الطوائف زي "الشيالين" و"الصنايعية" و"الجرسونات" و"الموظفين" و"السقايين" وكمان أغانيه التانية زي "ضيعت مستقبل حياتي" و"أنا هويت" ويا بهجة الروح" و"خفيف الروح."
مات في ١٥ سبتمبر سنة ١٩٢٣ وهو عنده ٣١ سنة بس.

شادية

فنّانة مصريّة مشهورة. اتولدت في القاهرة في فبراير سنة ١٩٣٤. لقّبها الجمهور والنقّاد بـ"دلوعة السينما." قدّمت في حوالي ٤٠ سنة ١١٢ فيلم و١٠ مسلسلات إذاعيّة ومسرحيّة واحدة. وهي في نظر نقّاد كتير أهم فنانة شاملة في تاريخ الدّراما العربية. اتجوّزت ٣ مرات وماخلّفتش خالص. بدأت مسيرتها الفنيّة من سنة ١٩٤٧ لحد سنة ١٩٨٤. اعتزلت الفنّ لما كان عندها ٥٠ سنة وهي في عزّ نجوميّتها. واتفرّغت لرعاية الأطفال الأيتام. من أشهر أفلامها "الزّوجة ١٣" و"زقاق المدق" و"لحن الوفاء" و"التّلميذة" و"مراتي مدير عام." ومن أشهر أغانيها "الحب الحقيقي" و"بسبوسة" و"اتعوّدت عليك" و"إن راح منّك يا عين" و"آه يا أسمراني اللون."

صلاح جاهين

شاعر ورسّام كاريكاتير وصحفي مصري راحل. اتولد في القاهرة في ديسمبر ١٩٣٠. اتجوّز صلاح جاهين مرتين وخلف تلات أولاد، ولدين وبنت. أنتج بعض الأفلام اللي نجحت واعتبرت من علامات السّينما المصريّة زي "عودة الابن الضّال" و"أميرة حبّي أنا." كمان كتب وشارك في سيناريو وحوار بعض الأفلام منها "أميرة حبي أنا" و"خلي بالك من زوزو" و"شفيقة ومتولي" و"المتوحّشة." ومثّل في بعض الأفلام زي "اللص والكلاب" و"لا وقت للحب." وكانت قمة إبداعاته الشعريّة "الرّباعيّات" اللي لحنها سيد مكّاوي وغنّاها علي الحجّار. ألّف أكتر من ١٦١ قصيدة. وكتب أوبريت "الليلة الكبيرة" أشهر أوبريت للعرايس في مصر. فارق الحياة في أبريل ١٩٨٦.

عادل عمر

شاعر مصري. بدأت أعماله في الظهور مع الملحن أحمد منيب في أغنية "بحبك كون" اللي غناها علاء عبد الخالق سنة ١٩٨٦. اتعرف على حميد الشاعري ولحن له أشعار كتير. بلغت أعماله حوالي ٤٠٠ أغنية تقريبًا، غنى معظمها مطربي الموسيقى الحديثة زي عمرو دياب وإيهاب توفيق وفارس وهشام عباس وحميد الشاعري. من أشهر أعماله "داني" و"أول مرة" و"لو" و"مساكين" و"ولا عمري" و"قمر قمر" و"ويلوموني" و"العيون."

عبد الرحيم منصور

شاعر مصري مشهور. من أهم أغانيه "الله أكبر بسم الله" غناء المجموعة، "على الربابة" لوردة، "باعشق البحر" لنجاة، "يا عشقنا" و"إن كنت ليا وأنا ليك" لشادية، "حبيبي يا متغرب" لفايزة أحمد، و"ألوان" لعماد عبد الحليم. كتب أغاني وأشعار فيلم "الزمار" ومسلسل "مارد الجبل." صدر له ديوان "الرقص ع الحصى." قدم مع الملحن أحمد منيب الفنان محمد منير وآخرين، وشارك الملحن بليغ حمدي في إعادة تقديم أغاني الفلكلور. أصدرت الهيئة العامة للكتاب كتابًا يجمع كل أعماله الشعرية من إعداد ابنة أخيه مي منصور سنة ٢٠١٥. توفي في ٢٨ يوليو سنة ١٩٨٤.

عبد العظيم عويضة

ملحن اتولد سنة ١٩٣٨. درس الموسيقى في الكونسيرفتوار ولحن بعض المسرحيات لمسرح الطليعة. وكون فريق للغناء الجماعي سنة ١٩٦٨ يغني أغاني وطنية وقت معارك الاستنزاف مع إسرائيل. لحن بعض أعمال الشاعرين فؤاد حداد وصلاح جاهين. من أشهر أعماله "الجيرة والعشرة" و"فين الحقيقة يا خال" و"الحقيقة والميلاد" و"الناس نامت" و"عينيكي تحت القمر" لمحمد منير.

عبد الفتاح مصطفى

شاعر مصري معروف. اتولد في القاهرة سنة ١٩٢٤ واتخرج من كلية الحقوق سنة ١٩٤٧. وحصل على دبلوم في الشريعة الإسلامية. بدأ الكتابة في الإذاعة مع الملحن أحمد صدقي. قدم مع أم كلثوم بعض

الأغاني الوطنية والدينية والعاطفية زي "طوف وشوف" و"يا حبنا الكبير" و"منصورة يا ثورة الأحرار" و"أقول لك إيه عن الشوق" و"لسه فاكر" و"ليلي ونهاري." كتب بعض الأوبريتات زي "حلم ليلة صيف" و"البيرق النبوي." وكتب أغاني فيلم "الشيماء" وسيناريو وحوار فيلم "أمير الدهاء." كتب كلمات ١٠ أدعيا لعبد الحليم حافظ. توفي سنة ١٩٨٤.

عزيز الشافعي

مؤلف وملحن ومغني مصري. لحن أغاني كتير لمطربي العالم زي تامر حسني ونيكول سابا ومحمد فؤاد وخالد سليم وإيهاب توفيق وهيفاء وهبي. من أشهر أعماله كملحن أغنية "ما تزعليش يا مصر" سنة ٢٠٠٩ لهشام عباس اللي فازت بجايزتين سنة ٢٠٠٩ و٢٠١٠. ومن أشهر أغانيه كمان اللي كتب كلماتها ولحنها أغنية "يا بتاع النعناع" اللي غناها مصطفى حجاج سنة ٢٠١٥.

عمرو دياب

مطرب مصري معاصر. من مواليد أكتوبر ١٩٦١ في بور سعيد. حقَّقت ألبوماته مبيعات هائلة واتَرجمت أغاني كتير له للغات كتير زي الإنجليزي والتَركي والرُوسي والهندي. تميَّز عمرو دياب بإدخال آلات جديدة في أغانيه. سنة ١٩٨٢ انتقل للقاهرة والتحق بالمعهد العالي للموسيقى العربية. غنَّى في افتتاح دورة الألعاب الأفريقيَة في استاد القاهرة سنة ١٩٩٠ أغنية "أفريقيا" بالعربي والإنجليزي والفرنساوي وكان ده بداية طريقه للعالمية. حصل على عدة جوائز، بعضها أكتر من مرة زي جايزة الميوزيك أووردز (Music Awards). قدَّم أغنيَتين مع مطربين عالمين همَّ الشاب خالد في أغنية "قلبي" والمطربة اليونانيَة أنجيلا ديمتريو في أغنية "أنا بحبَك أكتر." من أشهر أغانيه "تملي معاك" و"نور العين" و"قمرين" و"وهي عاملة إيه دلوقت" و"رجعت من السَفر."

عمرو مصطفى

ملحن ومغني مصري. اتولد سنة ١٩٧٨ في القاهرة. ظهر حبه للموسيقى من الطفولة فكان بيلحن القصايد العربية الموجودة في كتب العربي في المدرسة. لحن لأشهر المطربين العرب زي مصطفى قمر ومحمد منير وهشام عباس ونوال الزغبي. حصلت كتير من ألبوماته على جوايز أهمها الـ World Music Awards. أصدر تلات ألبومات كمغني من سنة ٢٠٠٧. شارك عمرو مصطفى كضيف شرف في فيلم "بحبك وأنا كمان" مع مصطفى قمر. صور عمرو مصطفى تلات كليبات هي "لو في حياتي" و"برتاح معاك" و"أول ما أقول."

عمَّار الشَّريعي

موسيقار ومؤلف وناقد مصري. اتولد في المنيا في صعيد مصر في أبريل ١٩٤٨. له علامات وبصمات في الموسيقى الآلية والغنائية المصرية، بالإضافة للموسيقى التَصويريَة للأفلام والمسلسلات التَلفزيونيَة رغم إنه كفيف. حصل على ليسانس الآداب قسم إنجليزي من جامعة عين شمس سنة ١٩٧٠. بدأ حياته العمليَّة كعازف لآلة الأكورديون في عدد من الفرق الموسيقيَة اللي كانت منتشرة في مصر. بعد كده

تحول للأورج اللي بزغ نجمه فيه كأبرع العازفين في جيله. اهتم بتقديم أغاني الأطفال وغنّى من ألحانه في المجال ده مطربين كتير زي عفاف راضي وعبد المنعم مدبولي ونيللي وصفاء أبو السعود. اهتمَّ كمان بتقديم مواهب جديدة في الغُنى زي هدى عمّار وريهام عبد الحكيم. اتعيّن كأستاذ غير متفرغ بأكاديمية الفنون المصريّة سنة ١٩٩٥. تجاوزت أعماله السينمائيّة كمؤلف موسيقى ٥٠ فيلم وأعماله التلفزيونيّة ١٥٠ مسلسل وأكثر من ٢٠ عمل إذاعي. قدّم برنامج مشهور اسمه "غوّاص في بحر النَغم." أُصيب بأزمة قلبية نتيجة الإرهاق وتوفي في ٧ ديسمبر ٢٠١٢.

عوض بدوي

شاعر مصري من الإسكندرية. اتخرج من جامعة الإسكندرية. بدأ طريقه للفن من خلال والده اللي كان بيحب الشعر والأدب. غنى من أعماله وردة الجزائرية "عدت سنة،" وعفاف راضي، ومحمد منير "عشقك ندى،" ومصطفى قمر، وفارس، ونانسي عجرم "شخبط شخابيط،" ومدحت صالح، وهشام عباس، وحميد الشاعري، وجورج وسوف "يوم الوداع،" وإيمان البحر درويش "أنا طير في السما" و"أنا ماقبلش" وغيرهم.

كمال الطويل

ملحن ومؤلف موسيقى مصري راحل. اتولد في طنطا في أكتوبر ١٩٢٣. كان صديق الفنان عبد الحليم حافظ والموسيقار محمد الموجي. بعد دراسته الثانويّة سافر للقاهرة وبدأ طريق الفنّ. تُعتبر ألحانه اللي غنّاها عبد الحليم حافظ أشهر وأجمل ألحانه وهمّ اتقابلوا في ٥٦ أغنية عاطفيّة ووطنيّة. من أشهر أعماله "بالأحضان" و"والله زمان يا سلاحي" و"أحلف بسماها" و"سمراء" و"مطالب شعب" و"برّه الشبابيك." رحل عن عالمنا في يوليو ٢٠٠٣.

كمال منصور

شاعر مصري من مواليد محافظة الشَرقية في ١٢ فبراير ١٩٢٢. اتخرج من كلية الآداب. اشتغل في وزارة التربية والتعليم وجريدة أخبار اليوم. من أعماله "ماما يا حلوة" لشادية ومن ألحان منير مراد، و"حكايتي كانت وياك حكاية" لمحمود الشريف، و"نشيد أرض الجزائر" لعبد الحليم حافظ ومن ألحان بليغ حمدي. كتب الأغنية الدينية والعاطفية وكمان النشيد وكان واحد من اللي بشروا المبشرين بثورة يوليو خلال كتاباته الغنائية. كرمته دولة قطر عن النّشيد الوطني القطري. حصل على وسام الاستحقاق من الرئيس الجزائري الأسبق أحمد بن بلّة لما كتب أغنية "قضبان حديد" اللي غناها عبد الحليم حافظ. رحل عن دنيانا في ١٨ أكتوبر ١٩٨٩ وهو عنده ٦٧ سنة.

مأمون الشناوي

مأمون الشناوي (١٩١٤-١٩٩٤) هو واحد من أهم شعراء مصر ويعتبر من جيل الرواد، وهو من مواليد مدينة المنصورة. قدر يرضي كل الأذواق بقلمه. كمان له الفضل في إعادة صياغة أغاني الفلاحين والأغنيات الشَعبيّة الفلكلوريّة المصريّة. وهو أخو المؤلف كامل الشناوي. كان الشاعر الراحل بيتحمس

للمطربين والموسيقيين الجدد ويساعد في تقديمهم للساحة الفنية وكان بيكتب لهم مخصوص.

غنّت أم كلثوم من أشعاره أربع أغاني عاطفية هي "أنساك يا سلام" سنة ١٩٦١، "كل ليلة وكل يوم" سنة ١٩٦٤، "بعيد عنك" سنة ١٩٦٥، وكلها من ألحان بليغ حمدي، وأغنية "ودارت الأيام" سنة ١٩٧٠ من لحن محمد عبد الوهاب. اتعاون مأمون الشناوي مع الموسيقار محمد عبد الوهاب في عدد من الأغاني العاطفية كان أولها "إنت وعزولي وزماني" عام ١٩٤١، بعد كده "ردي عليا" من فيلم "ممنوع الحب،" و"انسى الدنيا" من فيلم "رصاصة في القلب،" و"آه منك يا جارحني،" و"على بالي،" و"قابلته،" و"كل ده كان إيه كنا هنا." كما عملوا مع بعض عدد من الأغاني الوطنية زي نشيد "الوادي،" و"زود جيش أوطانك،" و"الجهاد." وغنى فريد الأطرش مجموعة من أجمل أغانيه زي "حبيب العمر،" و"بنادي عليك،" و"أول همسة،" و"الربيع،" و"حكاية غرامي،" و"خليها على الله،" و"سافر مع السلامة،" و"نجوم الليل،" و"جميل جمال،" و"يا قلبي يا مجروح،" و"ماتقولش لحد،" و"لحن حبي،" و"طال غيابك،" و"أنا كنت فاكرك ملاك،" و"إنت اللي كنت بادور عليك،" و"أنا واللي باحبه،" و"تقول لا،" و"سنة وسنتين،" و"هافضل أحبك،" و"ليه دايمًا ماعرفش،" و"أنا وإنت والحب كفاية علينا،" و"ماقدرش أقول آه،" و"الحب لحن جميل،" و"باحبك إنت." وغنى له عبد الحليم حافظ "أنا لك على طول" و"عشانك يا قمر" من ألحان محمد عبد الوهاب، "بيني وبينك إيه" و"صدفة" و"نعم ياحبيبي نعم" و"في يوم من الأيام" و"كفاية نورك عليا" و"حلَفني" و"بعد إيه" من ألحان كمال الطويل، "أقول ماقولشي" و"لو كنت يوم أنساك" من ألحان محمد الموجي، "خايف مرة" و"خسارة خسارة" من ألحان بليغ حمدي، و"حلو وكداب" من لحن محمود الشريف. ألف مأمون الشناوي لعبد الحليم حافظ أغاني وطنيّة زي "إني ملكت في يدي زمامي" من لحن كمال الطويل، و"ثورتنا المصريّة" من لحن رؤوف ذهني. ألف لأسمهان في فيلم "غرام وانتقام" عام ١٩٤٤ أغنيتين هم "قهوة" و"إمتى هتعرف." كمان ألف لليلى مراد أغنية "ليه خلتني أحبَك" من لحن كمال الطويل، وألف لفايزة أحمد "تهجرني بحكاية" و"بصراحة" والاتنين من لحن محمد عبد الوهاب.

محمد حمزة

شاعر غنائي مصري راحل. اتولد في يونيو ١٩٤٠. بدأ كتابة الشّعر الغنائي باحتراف سنة ١٩٦٣ لمّا قدّمته فايزة أحمد في أغنية "أومر يا قمر" لحد ما وصل رصيده لـ١٢٠٠ أغنية. عمل كصحفي وناقد في بعض إصدارات روز اليوسف وصباح الخير والوفد. أشهر أعماله "أي دمعة حزن لا" و"موعود" و"مدّاح القمر" اللي غنّاها عبد الحليم حافظ و"حكايتي مع الزّمان" و"يا حبيبتي يا مصر." تُوفي في يونيو ٢٠١٠.

محمد عبد الوهاب

أشهر موسيقار مصري وعربي على الإطلاق. اتولد في القاهرة في مارس سنة ١٩٠٢. ولُقَب بـ"موسيقار الأجيال" لأنه ساند المطربين بألحانه طوال القرن العشرين. اشتغل في السّينما المصرية كملحّن ومطرب وممثّل. اتعلّم العود في معهد الموسيقى العربيّة على يد الملحّن الكبير محمد القصبجي. وعمل في نفس الوقت كمدرس للأناشيد في مدرسة الخازندار. وبدأ العمل في السّينما سنة ١٩٣٣ وفي الإذاعة سنة ١٩٣٤. تعهده أمير الشّعراء أحمد شوقي بالرّعاية وأحضر له مدرس للّغة الفرنسيّة وقدمه في الحفلات الفنيّة في مصر، وساعده في السّفر لفرنسا وهناك اتعرَف على أساليب الموسيقى

الغربيّة. لحن قصايد كتير من تأليف أحمد شوقي زي "دمشق،" و"النّيل نجاشي،" و"مضناك جفاه مرقده." مزج بين الموسيقى الشّرقيّة والغربيّة في ألحانه وقدّم إيقاعات غربيّة كتير في أغانيه وأعماله الموسيقيّة زي إيقاع الفالس في "الجندول" سنة ١٩٤١، وإيقاع الروك أند رول في طقطوقة "يا قلبي يا خالي" اللي غنّاها الفنان عبد الحليم حافظ سنة ١٩٥٧. تكاد تكون كل أعماله الموسيقيّة مشهورة بين المصريين والعرب، فهو قدّم أغاني في كل المجالات الغنائيّة تقريبًا فله الأغاني الرومانسيّة والوطنيّة والدينيّة والفلسفيّة. وله أعمال بالفصحى والعاميّة، وأغاني طويلة وقصيرة. أطول أغنيّة ممكن توصل لساعتين وأقصر أغنيّة ممكن تكون ٣ دقايق. لحن لمطربين من مصر ولبنان وسوريا والجزائر زي أم كلثوم وصباح وشادية ونجاة ووردة وأسمهان وفيروز وعبد الحليم حافظ ووديع الصّافي. ومن أعماله السينمائيّة "الوردة البيضاء" و"دموع الحب" و"يوم سعيد." حصل على جوايز كتير من مصر والدول العربيّة والأجنبيّة زي الجايزة التقديريّة في الفنون ونيشان النّيل والميداليّة الذهبيّة من مهرجان موسكو ووسام الاستحقاق السوري ووسام الأرز اللبناني، وحصل على الدّكتوراة الفخريّة من أكاديميّة الفنون سنة ١٩٧٥.

توفي في مايو ١٩٩١ نتيجة جلطة في المخ. وشُيّعت له جنازة عسكريّة مهيبة بناء على قرار الرئيس السّابق محمد حسني مبارك.

محمد منير

مغنّي معاصر مصري من أصل نوبي. اتولد في أسوان في أكتوبر سنة ١٩٥٤. اتعلّم وقضى فترة صباه في أسوان قبل ما يهاجر للقاهرة. اتخرّج من قسم الفوتوغرافيا من كليّة الفنون التّطبيقيّة بجامعة حلوان. اشتهر بأسلوب غناؤه وأداؤه الغير ملتزم بتقاليد الطّرب والمطربين، وبخاصة شعره النّامي المفلفل بفوضى. ارتبط بأشعار الصّفّ الأول من شعراء العاميّة المصريّة كعبد الرّحمن الأبنودي وعبد الرّحيم منصور وفؤاد حداد المغايرة للنبرة الرومانسيّة وموسيقاها المختلفة عن موسيقى الطّرب التقليدي. قدّم أغانيه باللهجتين القاهريّة والأسوانيّة وقدّم كمان بعض الأغاني النوبيّة. اشتهر في بدايته كمغني للمثقفين لكن في فترة التّسعينات قدر إنه يكسر الصّورة النّمطيّة دي ويبقى من المألوف سماع أغانيه في الشّارع. قام بأداء أغاني فيلم "المصير" سنة ١٩٩٦ من إخراج يوسف شاهين. قدّم ألبوم ديني كامل بعنوان "الأرض السّلام" سنة ٢٠٠٣. وغنّى تتر مسلسل الكرتون "بكّار." أهدى شباب ثورة ٢٥ يناير ٢٠١١ أغنية "إزاي." غطّت أغاني محمد منير معظم التّيمات الغنائيّة فمن أعماله الأغاني العاطفيّة والفلسفيّة والدينيّة والوطنيّة.

محمد يونس القاضي

شاعر مصري مشهور. اتولد في يونيو ١٨٨٨ في دمنهور. كان أبوه قاضي شرعي دخله الكتّاب وهو عنده ٤ سنين. دخل الأزهر وهو عنده ١٤ سنة. وظهرت مواهبه الشعرية والخطابية في المرحلة دي. كانت مسارح الفترة دي محتاجة لمؤلف فألف مسرحيات لمنيرة المهدية. من أعماله "أنا هويت" و"أنا عشقت"و"ضيعت مستقبل حياتي" و"زوروني كل سنة مرة" والنشيد الوطني المصري "بلادي بلادي" وكلها من ألحان الموسيقار سيد درويش. توفي في ٣٠ يوليو سنة ١٩٦٩.

مصطفى حجاج

مغني مصري اشتهر بأغنية "يا بتاع النعناع" سنة ٢٠١٥ اللي اتخطت المية مليون مشاهدة على موقع اليوتيوب. بدأ الغناء في الأفراح الشعبية وهو عنده تمن سنين. حصل على دبلوم الصنايع. اكتشفه المنتج نصر محروس وأنتج له أول ألبوم بعنوان "زحمة حياتي." سنة ٢٠١٦ أصدرت نقابة الموسيقيين قرار بوقف حجاج من الغناء بسبب عدم تأديته الخدمة العسكرية.

منتصر حجازي

شاعر مصري. شارك في تأسيس فريق "وسط البلد" في أواخر التسعينات وكتب أغاني للفريق لفترة طويلة امتدت عشرين سنة لغاية دلوقتي، وكانت أول أغنية ليهم هي "هيلاهوب" سنة ٢٠٠١. واتعاون كمان مع فرقة المدينة ومن أشهر أغانيهم "أنا مفلس وجايب جاز." صدر له عدد من الدواوين الشعرية بالعامية المصرية. كما كتب أغاني فيلم "تيتو" بطولة أحمد السقا.

منير مراد

منير مراد (١٩٢٠-١٩٨١) ملحن وممثل مصري كان يهودي وأسلم. وهو أخو الفنانة ليلى مراد واتجوز الفنانة سهير البابلي. وهو فنان متعدد المواهب، اتميز في مجال التلحين للأغنيات الخفيفة والمرحة، ولحن أكتر من دويتو يجمع الفنانة شادية والفنان عبد الحليم حافظ. قام في بداية حياته ببطولة عدد من الأفلام السينمائية كان أشهرها "نهارك سعيد."
غنت شادية من ألحانه "إن راح منك يا عين،" "ألو ألو،" "إوعى تسيبني،" "اسم الله عليك،" "الدنيا مالها،" "تعالى أقولَّك،" "حاجة غريبة،" "دوَّر عليه،" "سوق على مهلك،" "شبك حبيبي،" "ماقدرش أحب اتنين،" "يا سارق من عيني النَوم،" "يا دبلة الخطوبة،" "لسانك حصانك،" "يا دنيا زوقوكي،" "وعد ومكتوب،" "منايا أغني،" "يا حبيبي عود لي تاني،" "مش قلت لك يا قلبي." لحن كمان لأشهر المطربين العرب زي عبد الحليم حافظ وصباح ووردة ومحمد رشدي ومحرم فؤاد. توفي منير مراد في ١٧ أكتوبر ١٩٨١ عن عمر يناهز الـ٦٠ سنة.

ناصر المزداوي

هو موسيقي ليبي من مواليد ١٩٥٠ في مزدة في ليبيا. اتخرَّج من معهد جمال الدين الميلادي للموسيقى في طرابلس. بيعرف عربي وإنجليزي وإيطالي وفرنساوي، وهو عازف على آلات القيثارة والعود والكمان والبيانو. بدأ ناصر المزداوي في المجال الفني من نهايات الستينات وعمل خلالها بعض الحفلات في بلاد كتير زي المكسيك وكوبا وبريطانيا وأمريكا والبرازيل واليونان وبعض البلاد العربية. قدم مجموعة من الألحان لعدد من الفنانين العرب بينهم حميد الشاعري وعمرو دياب زي أغنية "كمَل كلامك" وأغنية "نور العين."

نانسي عجرم

مغنية لبنانية من مواليد سنة ١٩٨٣ بقرية سهيلة، بمحافظة جبل لبنان. حاصلة على أكتر من جايزة بلاتينية وفايزة بتلات جوايز موسيقية عالمية. اشتهرت بأغنيها المصورة، وشكلت ثنائي ناجح مع المخرجة اللبنانية نادين لبكي في أغاني اشتهرت على الصعيد اللبناني والعربي، زي "أخاصمك آه،" "يا سلام،" "آه ونص،" "يا طبطب يا دلع،" "شَخُبط شَخابيط،" "بتفكر في إيه." في أوائل القرن الواحد والعشرين عملت صفقات إعلانية مع شركات كوكا كولا ودماس للمجوهرات وسوني إريكسون. سنة ٢٠٠٣ أطلقت ألبومها التالت "يا سلام" المتضمن أغنية "أخاصمك آه" كان سبب انطلاقها وشهرتها وضم الكليب الخاص بها رقصات إثارة وإغراء، أمَا كليبات "يا سلام" و"ياه سحر عيونه" فكانوا كليبات رومانسية عاطفية. وسنة ٢٠٠٦ أطلقت أغنية منفردة اسمها "إنت مصري" تزامنًا مع بطولة كأس الأمم الأفريقية وحققت الأغنية شهرة بالرغم إن كلمات الأغنية مش متعلقة بالرياضة. في يونيو ٢٠٠٧ أطلقت ألبوم "شخبط شخابيط" اللي خصصت أغانيه للأطفال. سنة ٢٠٠٨ أطلقت ألبومها "بتفكر في إيه" وصورت لأغانيه كذا كليب زي "بتفكر في إيه،" "لمسة إيد،" "ابن الجيران،" و"ماشي حدي." فازت بجايزة ورلد ميوزك أوووردز (World Music Awards) سنة ٢٠٠٨ عن ألبومها "بتفكر في إيه" بعد ما حققت مبيعات عالية بوقت قياسي. وسنة ٢٠١٠ أطلقت ألبومها التامن "نانسي ٧" والألبوم ده حقق مبيعات ٥ مليون نسخة في وقت قصير جدًا وحققت رقم قياسي تاني، وخدت جايزة الورلد ميوزك أوووردز للمرة التانية لسنة ٢٠١١.

نصر الدين ناجي

شاعر مصري معاصر. يعتبر من أهم شعراء جيله في تغيير نمط كتابة الأغنية في مصر. اتولد في مدينة المحلة الكبرى بمحافظة الغربية. انتقل لمدينة الإسكندرية عشان يدخل كلية التربية الرياضية بجامعة الإسكندرية، بعد كده انتقل للقاهرة واحترف كتابة الشعر الغنائي. بدأ مشواره الفني بالتعامل مع المطرب الكبير محمد منير في ألبوم "طعم البيوت" بتلات أغنيات كانت بداية انطلاق اسمه الفني في عالم الغناء وهي "طعم البيوت" و"من غير كسوف" و"كان فاضل." وتوالت أعماله الفنية بعد كده واتعامل مع كتير من الفنانين المصريين وغير المصريين زي مصطفى قمر وسميرة سعيد وأنغام. وهو رايد في كتابة الأغنية الدعائية للعديد من الشركات المعلنة. واتجه مؤخرًا لكتابة ديوانه الأول واسمه "عايش لحد ما أموت."

هاني شنودة

ملحن مصري معروف. اتولد سنة ١٩٤٣ في طنطا. درس الموسيقى في معهد الكونسيرفتوار قسم "تأليف وإيقاع." وكانت والدته بتعزف على البيانو والعود. في القاهرة كون كذا فرقة موسيقية غنائية كان في آخرهم ٣ عازفين على الكي بورد (keyboard) لأول مرة في مصر. غنى من أعماله عمرو دياب ومحمد ثروت ولبلبة. لحن أول برنامج للأطفال سنة ١٩٧٠ تأليف شوقي حجاب، ووزع ألبوم "علموني عينيك" بتاع محمد منير، وعمل الموسيقى التصويرية لـ٣٠٠ فيلم منها "المشبوه" و"غريب في بيتي" و"عصابة حمادة وتوتو" و"المولد."

وليد سعد

ملحن مصري مشهور. من مواليد الإسماعيلية في ١٨ فبراير عام ١٩٧٣. نشأ في أسرة فنية، فوالده هو الفنان حسن سعد، مطرب السمسمية الأول، واللي مثّل مصر بحفلاته وأغنياته في كل أنحاء العالم. اتأثر وليد بوالده كتير واعتبره معلمه الأول، وزرع فيه أبوه من الصغر حب الموسيقى. دخل المعهد العالي للموسيقى العربية بناء على نصيحة والده، عشان يصقل موهبته بالدراسة الأكاديمية. حصل على بكالوريوس المعهد العالي للموسيقى العربية سنة ١٩٩٣ بتقدير امتياز مع مرتبة الشَرف، وترتيبه كان الأول على الدفعة. اتعين بعد تخرجه معيد في المعهد العالي للموسيقى العربية لكنه فضّل الابتعاد عن العمل الأكاديمي والتفرغ للتلحين والغناء.

بدأ مشواره مع الاحتراف سنة ١٩٩٤ بأول أغنية من ألحانه "أول حبيب" للمطرب إبراهيم عبد القادر وبعد كده أغنية "أوعدك" للمطرب أحمد جوهر، وأغنية "يا راميني في الغرام" لهشام عباس، وبعدها توالت أعماله الناجحة مع جميع نجوم مصر والوطن العربي. قدر وليد سعد إنه يكون في مصاف كبار ملحنين الوطن العربي ويقدم مئات من الألحان الناجحة. خد جوايز كتير في كتير من الاستفتاءات، ونال التكريم من كذا مؤسسة فنية وإعلامية في مصر والوطن العربي.

من أعماله "لو كان يرضيك" و"لسه بتحبه" لعمرو دياب، و"خايف" و"بتبعديني" لمحمد منير، و"شكرًا" لجورج وسوف، و"غريبة النَّاس" لوائل جسار، و"قابلتك ليه" لسميرة سعيد، و"مش حبيبة حد فينا" لمحمد فؤاد، و"جرحني مرة" لبهاء سلطان.